STUCK ON A
FERRIS WHEEL

AN ACTOR'S GUIDE TO ENJOYING THE RIDE
WHILE KEEPING YOUR FEET ON THE GROUND

by
Abbie Cobb

Stuck on a Ferris Wheel

An actor's guide to enjoying the ride while keeping your feet on the ground

Edited by
Heather and Michael Colletto
collettostories.com

Cover Design by Dani Snell
danisnell.com

Illustrations by Kassandra Gamez
kozispoon.blogspot.com

Table of Contents

About This Book I

Let's Get Started...................................III

Chapter One: Planning the Trip...........1

Chapter Two: Headshots....................15

Chapter Three: Resumés....................29

Chapter Four: Making a Reel.............41

Chapter Five: Representation............51

Chapter Six: Auditions........................61

Chapter Seven: Voiceover Work.....105

Chapter Eight: Marketing.................113

Chapter Nine: Getting Paid.............135

Chapter Ten: Unions 101.................141

Chapter Eleven: The Spiritual Side of Things...............................157

Closing...............................183

Glossary 185

About This Book

There are several sections scattered throughout this book that I'd like you to be aware of as you're reading:

What You Can Do Right Now

Why wait? This section will list things you can start working on while you're sitting at home in Wahoo, Nebraska. If you get an early start on these suggestions, you'll find yourself ahead of the game when you're ready to make your move. Don't count yourself out of the game just because you aren't already living in LA. In fact, it's important that you do many of these things before even getting to Hollywood.

People You Should Know

Since I've moved to LA, I've come in contact with some fantastic industry professionals, websites, showcases, classes, etc. I'd love to share these connections with you to save you some time and money and make sure you're getting the quality help you deserve! I can't guarantee any of them, but they have worked for me in the past.

The Time I Failed At...

I ain't perfect, people. I've made some gigantic mistakes while pursuing this dream, and I thought I'd help you by sharing my flops. Laugh all you want. Seriously! Just don't do what I did.

Glossary

Let's face it. There are some ridiculous industry terms out there. It would be plain silly of me to assume that you know them all when a few short years ago I was perfectly clueless! Sides? Mark? 2nd 2nd? What the what? The glossary is there for you in case you come across a term you do not recognize. Use it and thank your school librarian for teaching you how to use it.

Let's Get Started

When I first moved to Los Angeles to pursue my dream of being an actor, one of the very first jobs I landed was as an extra in the film *When A Stranger Calls*. I was pumped! I arrived on set at 8 p.m., ready to begin the night shoot as the best "carnival go-er" I could be.

I couldn't believe that I would be paid to ride rides all night long—incredible! I was assigned to ride the giant Ferris wheel, so I grabbed some real cotton candy and some fake tickets and headed to board the ride.

As I climbed onboard, I was surprised by a bit of movie magic: my Ferris wheel partner was a dummy. Like, a literal dummy. (Dummies are typically cheaper and less demanding than actors.) My job was to throw my arms in the air every so often to make it appear that the ride was full and we were real passengers.

All was well and good. It was a lovely date with the dummy, some cotton candy, and me. Making money at an amusement park? Priceless. Time passed quickly and soon it was 2 a.m.—time for our first official meal break. The Ferris wheel operator, who was an actor sporting fake tattoos from the wardrobe department, began to let people off to go to the catered meal that production was providing for us down the street. As everyone got off the ride, leaving their dummy behind, the carts rotated around the wheel, one by one.

When I was at the top, I looked out to see all of Los Angeles. The lights of downtown were mesmerizing. Some stars had come out and were peeking out from behind the skyscrapers. How lucky I was to be at the top of this ride, in the middle of the night! I gazed at palm trees and couldn't believe I was in one of the most glorious cities in the world.

Soon, I'm going to be a real actress, I thought. I watched my fellow starry-eyed actors make their way across the carnival grounds towards the food. I can't believe I'm going to eat a catered meal... Hey, there's the ride oper—Uh oh.

I had wondered why the carts weren't moving any longer. There was the ride operator, walking happily away from the Ferris wheel, on his way to some free food. There he went, around the corner and out of sight.

I was stuck at the top of the Ferris wheel. In the middle of the night. In the middle of Los Angeles. He thought I was a dummy.

IV

And, boy, did I feel like one. It's not hard to feel like a dummy in this town. I don't want you to make the same mistakes I made. I don't want you to be stuck.

Frankly, I was so tired of there not being material available on simply how to get started in Los Angeles. I often read acting books and was puzzled as to why so many began with auditioning for a major network or signing contracts. If you're just starting out in this industry, thinking about starting, or have started but you've been stalled a bit, you can't just go and audition for networks. What about agents? What about doing non-Equity theatre? Sure, you have problems when you're about to audition for NBC, but I was dying to know how to go about *getting* there so I could begin to have network problems of my own!

It was also tricky to find a book that spoke about morality in the entertainment industry. I wish I had known what I know now about some of the decisions acting in LA would force me to make, both on a personal and professional level.

I've made a lot of mistakes as an actress in LA. I've been sidetracked and derailed more than a few times. But I've also learned a lot through them. When I would see an anxious fellow actor about to make the same mistakes I did, I jumped at the chance to help them skip out on the mess I had just made myself. I realized there were a lot more people who probably needed the information that I'd discovered and had wasted years learning by trial and error.

When I began my own journey several years ago, I was just a young student. Although I had a handful of talent, a big dream, and a lot of gumption, I didn't have a clue what I was getting myself into. I was a dummy. But after several years in this business, I'm making it. I haven't won an Oscar or an Emmy (yet!), but I am a working actor. And I got here by trial and error, hard work, and a lot of faith.

I did eventually get off that Ferris wheel about two hours later when the crew returned from their meal, their bellies full. My cotton candy, my sugar high, and my enthusiasm were long gone at that point, but I survived. This wasn't the last time I'd get stuck in my quest for success in Hollywood. Not on a Ferris wheel, thankfully, but that Ferris wheel became a symbol in my head for the endless circles we little actors run in trying to figure out what on earth we're doing.

If you want to get started in this business, you'll have to work hard. No book is going to take the hard work out of making it in Hollywood. But I can try to eliminate a lot of the guesswork and confusion that made my own journey so tough when I was just starting out. You don't have to be stuck on a Ferris wheel. You don't have to be a dummy.

Maybe you've wanted to be an actor since you watched *Ninja Turtles* as a four-year old. Or maybe the craving started just yesterday when you attended a Broadway show with your grand-children. Maybe you've always been somewhat interested, but you're just not sure how you could ever pursue acting while still maintaining your moral standards. This book is for you.

Chapter One
Planning the Trip

So you're ready to go! You've packed your suitcase and determined the length of time you'll be in LA, be it weeks, months, or forever. You know your first step is to land at LAX and catch a ride...but to where? And when you get there, what should you do first? Do you sign up for acting classes and then get a headshot? Should you look for an agent first or get a job to pay rent? There are some gray areas about what to do and when to do it, but here are my thoughts on the order and importance of things you need to do once you make it this far.

What Do I Need?

Savings

Visiting or moving to LA is going to be an investment. In addition to your apartment security deposit and first month's rent, there are a lot of upfront costs *and* continued costs associated with the business of being an actor. Later in this chapter, I detail the costs of living, working, and making it here in LA.

Car

Los Angeles isn't laid out like New York City. It's like nine cities spread out over many, many miles. It's possible to take the bus system, but buses aren't always reliable and can add hours to your commute. It isn't a guarantee that you will be able to find a route that will take you to the casting office you need to get to, especially if you're given an appointment on short notice. A car is a must.

Passion

I strongly encourage you to sit down, put your electronics away, and have a good, long brainstorming session about exactly why you want to come to LA. Is it for the money? Consider that, statistically, you'd be lucky to book a paying gig in the first three years that you're in LA—not to mention the taxes and commission that would come out of your paycheck. Is it for fame? Think about the fact that only 5 percent of people who call themselves "actors" in LA can survive on acting alone. And just because they're working actors doesn't mean we know their name. Your reasons better have something to do with crazy *passion* - passion that would make you crazy enough to pursue this tough industry with the full knowledge that you may not get paid for it and we may never know your name.

The (Suggested) Order of Events

1. Visit

The first thing you should do if you're considering a move to Los Angeles is to try to plan a visit to the city. Maybe you have an uncle or a cousin or a friend's friend whose couch you could crash on for a week or two. If you don't know anyone in the city, there are furnished apartments that you can rent by the week or the month (Google The Oakwood Apartments; they're great!) and some nice hotels that would provide a comfortable stay. If you fly to LA for the visit, you'll definitely need to rent a car while you are here. Along with getting all the tourist-y stuff out of the way, a visit is a great opportunity to get a feel for the city: traffic, weather, lifestyle, and neighborhoods. LA isn't for everyone. If you hate the area, it'd certainly be a good idea to know that before you pack up everything you own and move there. Don't you agree?

2. Find an Apartment

Studios and their casting offices are spread out all over LA, but you'll learn their locations and the best way to get there within a few weeks of auditioning steadily. Since you'll be driving all over the city, it's a good idea to be no more than a half-hour away from each major area. (Remember, a 30-minute drive in LA could be five miles. Yes, traffic is as bad as they say.) The majority of film and TV auditions occur (at least for me) in the following areas in this order:

- o Hollywood
- o Burbank
- o Santa Monica
- o West Hollywood
- o Studio City
- o Downtown (rare)
- o Woodland Hills (rare)

Most actors live in Hollywood or in the Valley. "The Valley" is short for The San Fernando Valley, which is north of Hollywood and between two major freeways, the 405 and the 5. It's broken up into Sherman Oaks, Van Nuys, Studio City, North Hollywood, Universal City, Toluca Lake, and Burbank. All of these areas are actor-friendly and provide a great community to live if you're a newbie. Hollywood is not in the Valley, but it is a bit cheaper and also close to audition sites. However, it can be a rougher part of town, depending on where your apartment is located; it might be cheaper, but you also might not want to walk around by yourself at night. Santa Monica is more expensive and further away, but the quality of living is nicer. It's a beach community with lots of tourists and doesn't have the suburban feel that the Valley does.

You'll want to avoid living downtown for your first stint in LA. It's far from almost all auditions, parking is impossible, and the rent is ridiculously high for a safe and clean apartment. Pasadena, Woodland Hills, Torrance, and Santa Clarita may prove to hold cheaper apartments, but they are farther away from the action. You'll find sitting in traffic day after day wears on you. The money you'll spend on gas may be more than what you're saving by living so far away.

If I had to choose the three safest and most comfortable areas for a new actor to live in, I would say to look for a place in Studio City, Toluca Lake, or Burbank.

3. Get a Survival Job
A survival job is your moneymaker. It's that sweet job with a steady paycheck that will allow you to pursue your craft. Bills have got to be paid! There are all kinds of creative solutions to

funding your crazy dream in the entertainment industry. The end goal, of course, is to get paid to do what you love—but, in the mean time, you have to have some money coming in to pay the rent, keep a car, and feed the cat. (Buying a cat is optional but personally recommended.)

I'm about to drop some honesty here. You will most likely not be booking any paying jobs in the first few weeks, or even the first few months, you are in LA. (I've known people who wisely gave themselves five YEARS to have zero expectations of a paycheck from acting!) And that's okay. That's what a survival job is for. If you're going to be smart about this move, you need to realize that not only will you be a fantastic actor seeking representation and comin' up with a banging headshot and marketing material, but you'll also be the best waitress on this side of the Mississippi, the handsomest bartender you ever did meet, or a baby-burpin' nanny and barista who coaches a weight training session before theatre rehearsal. You'll have mastered the art of the survival job.

You will blow through your savings faster than you could ever anticipate in this high-rent town. So hang up your ego, roll up your sleeves, and embrace the survival job smackdown.

A survival job should:

1. Be something you can stand (and even like!) because who knows how long it will take you to book steady paying gigs?
2. Give you the ability and flexibility to get out of work to attend a last-minute audition/callback/booking.

3. Provide enough income for you to comfortably pursue your craft. In other words, in addition to grocery money, you should have room in your budget to purchase marketing materials, take acting classes, etc. That's part of the business, too. But we'll get to that later.

Also, consider hunting down a job with health benefits. Several companies like Starbucks, Fed-Ex Office, UPS, Whole Foods and more currently offer health insurance coverage to part-time employees who work a certain number of hours per week or month.

You can say "see ya" to that restaurant hosting gig when you're finally bringing in enough income from your craft. That could mean you book a national commercial that covers a year's entire budget, you land a series regular on a TV show, or even doing two days of work on a feature film that pays bank. It will look a little different for everyone, but know that the long-term goal with a survival job is to eventually not need one.

4. Get Headshots
Okay, so you made it past the visit stage. You have a place to live and the survival job to pay for it. Congrats! Now on to the exciting creative stuff... pictures!

You'll want to schedule a photoshoot with a photographer who can offer quality headshots immediately. Your headshot is your ticket to the dance. Learn more about headshots—what to wear, where to get them, why they're so stinking important, etc.—in the next chapter.

5. Get Plugged In

Start seeking out groups to jump into right away. Building a support group to hold you up while you're here will guarantee that your time in LA lasts longer and will be infinitely more enjoyable. This is a big town with a lot of people, and you'll need friends. (Don't we all?) There are acting classes, generic entertainment industry mixers, faith-based groups, actor support groups, and even groups made up of people from your hometown. Never underestimate the value of community. You'll find which groups you'd like to try out on your own, with a little help from Google and new friends you meet when you've settled into your new apartment and survival job. (Throughout the book I also mention several that I'm a part of and recommend.)

6. Try to Find an Agent

An agent will be key to getting auditions and rocking out callbacks. It is important to know, though, that you'll first need a great headshot and the skills to excel at an audition before you'll have agents fighting to represent you. I will discuss how to get an agent in chapter five.

7. Audition
Until that agent comes along, audition your heart out by getting appointments on your own. Be sure to check out *Backstage West* right away (www.backstagewest.com*)*, check Craigslist regularly, and be sure to set up an account at actorsaccess.com. More on that in chapter six.

8. Breathe!
You made it. You're here! You dove in despite all the things that tried to keep you from this point. Take a deep breath and celebrate over a package of Ramen noodles. And share with your cat.

The Cost of the Trip and Staying
The prices I'm about to list are just estimates and will look entirely different depending on the situation, time of year, location, etc. They are just meant to give you a very general idea of typical costs. Also, it is important to fully understand your financial situation and budget, and then prioritize your spending accordingly. Hopefully the pricing information will be helpful, but do remember it is simply meant to be a guideline. This list does not include regular everyday things you'll need like a cell phone, food, car, gas, etc., so

make sure you account for these items in your budget, too. In terms of taxes, remember that spending on things like headshots and acting workshops will qualify as business expenses (which are a tax write-off).

Apartment: $800-$1,600 per month, depending on if you chose to go solo in a one-bedroom, have a roommate, indulge in a two-bedroom, etc. You also could get creative: I have a friend who pays a housemate $350 per month to sleep on the couch in the living room.

Headshots: $250-$650, depending on how many wardrobe changes you get, if a makeup/hair artist is included, and the quality of your photographer.

Reproducing headshots/postcards: $50-$200 each time you print, which could last you three months or three years. It all depends on how many you want to print, how many casting directors or agents you'd like to include in a mailing, and how many auditions you get! If you're *really* strapped for cash you can individually print headshots at FedEx or Walgreens for a few dollars a piece, but the quality and ability to customize your frame/name will be lacking. You'll definitely save money in the long run if you can print in bulk!

Acting service websites: $100-$200 per year. You'll need to subscribe to certain website services like actorsaccess.com, lacasting.com, and voice123.com depending on what kind of acting work you'd like to audition for.

Reel: a one-time fee of up to $600. This could be free if you gather up all the footage from projects you've done and already own and know how to use editing software. If not, you can purchase software for around $150 or hire a company to create a reel for you where they will film you doing several scenes as if from different hired projects and edit them together for you. There's a whole chapter on making reels (chapter four), so hold those questions for now.

Website: Anywhere from $12 up to a $1500 (one-time fee)! You'll have to buy or design a template when you create your site for the first time. This could be free if you have a buddy who can build web content for you upfront, or you could buy a pre-designed template from a place like yahoo.com for $35, or a more intricate template from a company like bludomain.com. Companies like WIX or WordPress are great if you have some tech knowledge, and they have plans were you can design and host for free, but to have your own domain name or to add extras will cost several bucks a month. Web hosting with an outside company like godaddy.com can be around $10-$25 per year. If you've got the smacks to spend and want to lay down a grand or two for a top-of-the-line site, there are definitely custom designers who will gladly do that for you. The sky is the limit with this one! More about websites in chapter 8.

Industry subscriptions: up to $200 a year, depending on what you find helpful. Some online subscriptions, like backstagewest.com and the casting director contact info available on castingabout.com, are invaluable.

Acting classes/workshops: $30-$100 on average per class, depending on the length of the class, the teacher, the casting director, etc.

Showcases: up to $5,000. Some local showcases are free and encourage you to bring friends that will pay a few bucks at the door to watch you perform. Some showcases are a week long at a fancy destination with six months of preparatory classes involved, which can be pricey, depending on the company.

PR announcements: $1-$4 per package. You can include a single postcard with a stamp for each announcement or you could do a postcard with some sort of gift in a bubble envelope plus postage, depending on your marketing plan.

What You Can Do Right Now

- o Start saving your money.
- o Figure out why you want to come. Write down your reasons!
- o Get out your calendar and begin to plan your first visit.
- o Analyze your car situation. If you have one, will it survive the drive to LA? Is it good for sitting in standstill traffic? If you don't have one, start researching online for a reliable car within your budget.
- o Check out apartment prices and locations in the LA area using services like craigslist.com, padmapper.com, etc.
- o Brainstorm possible survival jobs and work on a few connections. Jobs at places like Starbucks have a transfer program where you could work where you are and transfer to a location in another city once you're ready to make a move. There are several great companies like UPS, Starbucks, Whole Foods, Costco, Lowe's, etc. that have great health benefits and perks for their part-time employees.

Chapter Two
Headshots

As an actor, the first thing you need is a great headshot. Headshots are the single most important tool required to land a job. (You can even land a job without knowing how to act. Sad, but true.) So, before you put on your best get-up, get a haircut, and pose like you did on prom night, here are some thoughts and advice on what to do and what to avoid when it comes to headshots.

Know Your Type
Sorry, "talldarkandhandsome" is not the answer here. We're talking about *you*, who you truly are- and about how *knowing who you are* can work for you in an audition. No one knows you better than you, so why not help the casting directors out? Sometimes they have a very limited imagination. (The California sun can do that to you.) If the up-for-grabs role is a rebellious punk, don't come in dressed for your sweet sixteen party. (That is, unless you were a rebellious punk at sixteen.) If you're called in for a college frat boy/slacker-dude and you walk in wearing a tuxedo, then forget it. If you're called in for a James Bond type and you're sporting a worn

Green Day t-shirt and holes in your jeans, then forget it. You get the idea.

A list of potential types could go on forever, starting with your high school's cafeteria tables of cliques. Picture the types of characters that you see popping up in all kinds of major TV shows, print ads, commercials, and feature films.

Teacher
Lawyer
Babysitter
Stoner
Cheerleader
Bartender
Grandma
Band geek
Gamer

Doctor
Jock
Funny best friend
Prom King
Police Officer
Intern
Mom or Dad
Frat boy/sorority gal
Abused victim

Figure out what your type is and bring clothes that support your type! Even if you want to rebel against your type and be a Bond girl for once—and wouldn't we all?—remember that that might not be you! If you are overweight, embrace it; you will be the next millionaire booking roles as the funny best friend. If you are skinny and pale, embrace it; you're the next band geek in a *Glee* spinoff. If you're 22 and look 15, embrace it—you're in a lucrative category called "18 to look younger." For reasons involving everything from working laws to maturity levels, Disney loves filling their younger teen roles by casting actors who are not actually minors. Leonardo DiCaprio got started this way, and he has ended up at the top of the A-list. This happens to be my "type" as well (for now!), and learning to embrace the fact that I still look like a high school sophomore, instead of fighting that, has been key to landing several roles. Basically, figure out what you are and market yourself towards that type. Once you're rich and famous, you can play any part you want. For now, try to book a part that is your type. Your best fit is also your best shot.

Choosing a Photographer

How your headshots turn out is completely up to you! If you do the right amount of preparation, it can mean the difference between a failed attempt or complete success in Hollywood. Research photographers. Look at their work. Choose your clothes carefully. Put in time and careful thought about your type and your personality. At the photo shoot, do whatever you can to be yourself and be comfortable. Your face will sell it all. If your eyes are blank, your photo will be blank.

The Anatomy of a Headshot

There are a lot of unspoken rules when it comes to headshots. But they are very, very important unspoken rules. (That doesn't seem fair, does it?) Here are a few basic guidelines to put together a strong headshot:

Focus on your face. It would be a mistake for anything in your picture to pull the viewer's focus away from your face, your eyes, your smile (or lack of a smile). This is not a senior picture with your arms crossed because you're too cool for school. This is the real you!

Your head should be completely in the picture. A lot of photographers try to get artsy and take photos of you diagonally or cut the top part of your hair off. Not cool. Casting directors want to see your head. It's a headshot—the whole head should be in it! You can always crop the picture smaller when you're editing at home, but you can't add your hair back in (without mad Photoshop skills).

Leave your body out of it. Keep your hands (and torso) out of the picture. A headshot is your complete head, maybe some shoulders, maybe some arm, but not much more. Again, you don't want to distract the casting director. There are exceptions to every rule, but generally stay away from distant and zoomed-out photos for a headshot session. A more distant shot that includes your legs and torso is called a body-shot, which gives casting an idea of what size you are. This would be great for promotional projects, maybe for a postcard or a personal website, possibly for modeling jobs or for a role that may require nudity or bathing suit scenes. A body-shot is not a headshot.

The background should not be in focus. I've seen countless headshots of good-looking guys and girls standing there in beautiful wardrobe with a killer smile and the first thing I say when I see it is, "Wow, where was your photo shoot location? That is a cool background!" The casting director might think the same thing, and you don't want that slate-gray brick wall behind you to stand out more than your piercing blue eyes. You may find amazing locations, but you don't want them to outshine you. Your photographer should know this, but good lighting is more important than a cool-looking background. If you get a good shot back but the bricks or pipes or columns behind you are clearly in focus, you can blur them out in Photoshop. Anything to make your face pop out is key.

The background should not be the same color as your shirt. You want to stand out! Most likely the photographer has control over any backdrop color in their studio and already has any outdoor locations chosen. Make sure you show or tell them your shirt/dress colors before the shoot so you don't end up looking like a floating head when the pictures come back.

The photos really need to look like you—your personality, the *you* your friends see on a midnight run to Taco Bell, the smirk you give your significant other when they sass you, the stark emotion that hits you when the lyrics of a beautiful song hit home for the first time. The photo needs to capture your spirit, not just the contours of your face.

Do's and Don'ts

The following guidelines are what I have learned in workshops, conversations with professionals, photography classes, and in the smiles or frowns of the casting director in an audition room. Take them with a grain of salt, but I've found them to work fairly universally for acting in LA:

Wear jewel tones. This includes emerald greens, royal blues, deep purples, ruby red, etc. Don't wear pastels—they make you look weak and drab.

Wear the colors that complement you most for the shoot, and if you're not sure, ask your mom what she thinks is the best color on you. Trust me. If she hasn't told you already, she's dying to. If your skin is pale, avoid a color like yellow. If you're African-American and you know you can rock that canary yellow Banana Republic shirt you just bought, go for it. You know yourself. Trust it!

Complement your eye color. It sounds simple, but there are countless actors who have booked a job based on captivating eyes and their color brought out by a shirt or dress they were wearing. Do your research on what colors will make your eyes pop.

Make sure your clothes are ready to go. You don't want to be rushing around 10 minutes before the shoot. Iron them. Make sure they fit! Try them on and make sure they match the "type" you've chosen.

You can always pay someone to edit out the bags under your eyes, but who wants to do that? You *must* get a good night's sleep before your shoot. That sort of editing can be as much as $100 or more. You know what's cheaper? A few extra hours of sleep the night before your headshots. You need to be fresh and ready for the day!

Wear little to no jewelry. Necklaces are distracting! Only wear chains if they're part of your "look." Small earrings might go unnoticed but you may want to leave them behind. If you're married and under 25 or auditioning for someone young, leave your wedding ring at home; it will only make you seem older, tossing you from any teen or college opportunities. That being said, get your hands out of the shot!

Admit it: flannel is always distracting. Stripes might look great in a snapshot, but you don't want anything busy that draws any attention whatsoever to anything but your face. Forget the floral pattern. No writing on t-shirts. You may have a funny slogan or a cute hoodie with a brand name, but you don't want a casting director staring at your shirt, trying to figure out what that word is. You want him to be enamored with your eyes and on the phone with your agent to call you in for a read! (Now you can "know the rules to break the rules" here... if you've got a "Midwest Dad" look and think a bit of flannel works, then go for it. Just know my suggestions here apply most of the time.)

This isn't your wedding day or the prom. If a casting director sees a gorgeous picture of you sporting five pounds of makeup and a salon up-do, he'll be disappointed when you walk in the room looking like, well, you! Don't deceive them. The real you—natural and authentic—will get you more jobs than you think. So, what does that mean? Fix your hair like you could if you found out you had to be at an audition in 30 minutes—that means no help! Wear minimal makeup, only the basic coverage you need. Remember: these photos will be blown up into high-definition 8x10's and you can see makeup. If you're bald—show it! If you're overweight, don't try to hide it! Nothing will upset a casting director more than having you show up looking nothing like the headshot that they saw online.

Avoid drastic and last minute haircuts. What if it turns out badly? What if Tony the Barber has a bad day and slips up? (You should have tipped him last time, like Mama taught ya!) Photo shoots are too expensive and take too much planning to mess this up by depending on your stylist the day before. If you must get a cut or color, give yourself at least a week beforehand so that you have time to make any corrections if needed.

What You Can Do Right Now

- o Figure out your type.
- o Search for headshot photographers.
- o Save money for a worthy photographer!
- o Get in shape.
- o Floss daily and whiten your teeth.
- o Take care of acne.

The Time I Failed At...

Before making a long-term decision, I lived in LA for a summer as a trial run, just to make sure a film and TV career was what I wanted to pursue. I planned on getting new headshots taken at the beginning of my three-month stay, but I realized I had a box of over 100 shots leftover from my previous headshot session two years earlier. So I decided I should save my money and use up the extra headshots I had before buying new ones.

After about two weeks, I finally scored my first audition for a major TV show with my brand new agent. I was going to read for a guest star role on the show *Cold Case*. The episode revolved around a girl who was just starting out her freshman year, and she was made fun of by some stereotypical jerk athlete guys. The description of the character read that this role needed someone who was heavy-set. The script called for boys telling her she was "porky" or "piggy," and then she would cry in her room about all the teasing. Like I said: jerks.

Since the casting director calls you in based on your headshot alone, there was no way that they could've known I had lost a lot of weight since the picture was taken. (Farewell, Freshman Fifteen! Or, in my case, Thirty!) As I walked into the audition room and handed my headshot to the casting director, I saw the eyes roll and heard her sigh. I was completely wrong for the role. I was wasting my time, and, more importantly, I was wasting hers.

You absolutely must look like your headshot. Always. If your look changes, you absolutely must get new photos taken. If you happen to get a call for an appointment and you don't have your new photos online yet, it would be in your best interest to let the office know of the changes to your appearance up front (I lost all my hair, I'm now a blonde, I'm now in a wheelchair, I gained or lost thirty pounds, etc). It'd be far better for you to have an audition canceled than for you to show up and be hated.

People You Should Know

Photographers
Brian Parillo
brianparillophotography.com

Jason Tyler
www.hollywoodhillsheadshots.com

Printing
Headshot printing
www.reproductions.com

Postcards
www.uprinting.com/postcards

Business cards, postcards, stickers, etc.
www.gotprint.com

Chapter Three
The Resumé

Ah, the resumé. You'll find a billion different templates online and in books about creating the perfect acting resumé, but I've found a template I feel is the easiest and most universal. There are sections that won't apply to everyone, so take the parts that fit your goals and your experience and adjust it on your own.

Formatting the Resumé

Every resumé should have your name somewhere at the top in big bold letters. Your name should be larger than anything else on the page—left, right, or center.

If you are a member of a union, write some or all of the unions you are a part of in a top corner. If you're non-union, don't write anything. The only exception is if you're eligible to be in SAG-AFTRA (you've earned your three vouchers or you have had a line in a movie or TV show—discussed in chapter ten) but you haven't officially joined by paying your dues yet, write "SAG-E" or "SAG-ELIGIBLE" so people know you can join on a whim if you get offered a SAG role.

If you have an agent or manager (also called your "representation") that has a company logo, you can put their logo and phone number in a top corner as well. If your representation doesn't have a logo or you prefer not to use it, you can just put their name and phone number there instead. Add their office address and fax number only if you need to fill space. If you do not have representation, you can include your cell number and email address. If you have a website, list it somewhere at the top where you think it's noticeable but not cluttering your page.

There are a few schools of thought on putting your personal information on your resumé if you do have representation. Some say to always include a way for casting directors to contact you personally, just in case you change your representation. (My thought is you print out new resumés all the time, so that's not really a problem.) Others say to only include your representation's info because a casting office doesn't want to see your personal information on there. I combine the two: I have my agent and manager's phone numbers listed on the resumé, but I also have my website, which has a direct link to my email.

Just beneath the title, add your stats: height, eye color, and hair color. Include your date of birth only if you are under the age of 18. Once you're over 18, you don't want anyone knowing your age because it might affect their perception of your ability to play a certain look or role. Include your weight if there is a reason to, such as being overweight or very petite. Casting will need to know if you're one extreme or the other; if you're in the middle, your weight is probably irrelevant to casting decisions.

Note: If you're a model, listing weight and measurements is absolutely necessary. If you think you'll pursue acting as well as modeling, I would make sure you have a separate resumé solely for acting that does not have a long list of waist and bust sizes; casting directors for acting roles don't need to know those specifics unless they ask for them.

Now it's time for the good stuff! Begin listing your experience in several different performing categories: Film, TV, Theatre, Radio, Commercial, Modeling. Use whichever categories apply to you. For example, I do not have a dance category on my resumé because I don't have any dance credits to list. If one section is larger than the rest (more theatre credits than anything else, for example), then you'll generally want to put that at or near the top.

Remember that whatever category you decide to list at the top will be noticed first and probably remembered best. While my theatre section is bigger, I tend to meet more film and TV people in LA, so I created two resumés. When I audition for a play, I take the resumé that has theatre listed at the top; all other times, I take the resumé with the TV or Film section at the top.

You can also combine sections. I had one TV credit and five (student) film credits when I first created my resumé. I combined Film/TV together to have a section with six credits total in order to hide the fact that my TV section had one little credit all by its lonesome. Make sense? Note that it is best not to combine theatre with TV or Film, so that the person reviewing your resumé will know which roles are which with just a quick glance.

Create three columns. On the left, write the name of the show. The center column is for the character name or size of the role. Write the network, theatre, producer, or director on the right.

Here's an example for a theatre resumé:

Oliver!	Oliver	D. Sam Jones
Oklahoma	Lead	Clock Theatre
Camelot	Supporting	Whit Theatre
Macbeth	Ensemble	D. Mary Reed
Flowers	Chorus	Whit Theatre

A theatre resumé will be very similar to a television/film resumé. In the column listing your role, either write the name of the character or the size of the role, depending on how recognizable a character might be. For example, write the character name for Maria from *The Sound of Music*. That would be a great conversation starter! The character of Kurt Hummel on *Glee* was created and named because the actor they liked so much had previously performed in a play as Kurt, a major *Sound of Music* character. (They chose Hummel because they thought his red cheeks made him look like a Hummel figurine. True story. Now he has a Golden Globe.) If it's a play no one has ever heard of and/or a role most people would not be familiar with, then write the appropriate size of the role (lead, major supporting, supporting, ensemble, chorus, etc). You won't want to list character names for TV/Film, as the character names won't convey size of role like they would in famous theatre productions.

Think about what would be most recognizable for the third column as well. If it's a director people know, list their name. If it's a theatre that's known, list the theatre. Again, choose the word or name that most people would recognize and whatever would make that credit appear more professional. If you've done a production at a church or school, I advise you to leave off the "high school" or "church" part in the title of your theater because people may subconsciously judge that label as less professional. Even if you were cast out of thousands for the lead, they may immediately dismiss the production as not legitimate. Eliminate the negative assumptions at the get-go by leaving those labels off. For example, if you did theatre at Hickory Square High School, I would omit "High School" on that part of my resumé when listing my theatre performances there.

Also, do not feel the need to list your experience as a timeline. Unlike a standard work resumé, the chronological order of the roles does not matter. List each credit by order of importance or by size of role. What you list at the top will be seen first. Notice in the earlier example that I did not put all Whit Theater or director credits together. I placed them by the size of the role or acclaim of the show. Notice that "D. Their_name" or "Dir. Their_name" is an acceptable abbreviation of a director's title and name.

Here's an example for Film/TV:

Late Night	Lead	D. John Plum
Casey Goes	Lead	Red Pictures
SVU	Guest Star	D. Steve Lee
She Lives	Supporting	Li Production
CSI	Co-Star	CBS

Again, the name of the production is on the left. For this category, TV roles will either be Series Regular, Guest Star, or Co-Star. For film, it will be either "lead", "supporting lead", "supporting", or "dayplayer". On the right, the same is true as in theatre: list whatever is most recognizable. Mix up the credits by order of what you'd like the casting director to notice first. If the production company is well known, write it. If it's a channel people have heard of, such as Disney Channel or ESPN, list it by name. If it's the director's name that would catch attention, use it.

Remember that you want your best and brightest at the top of every column. If you have film and TV credits in the same section, it is okay to mix and match, putting your biggest roles at the top. You'll have TV and short films and independent films and student films all mixed up—which is a-okay!

Also, you don't have to write "student film" in the right-hand column. It may be true that you did a short film for some students, but they likely have a production name they've been required to make for their class. Ask them if they have a name they use for their films (what they use in the scrolling credits) or, at the very least, ask for the director's full name and use that name instead. Anyone looking at your resumé will assume that the films in your left-hand column are independent, short films, or student films if they aren't recognizable theatrical releases. Don't feel the need to call attention to that by labeling each type of film.

The Rest of Your Resumé

Unless you're an awesome superstar with more credits than Brad Pitt, you'll probably have room for another section or two. Consider choosing from the following: special skills, awards, hobbies, education, and training. These are pretty much self-explanatory. Special skills and training are the most common additional sections. You can put where you went to school or any additional industry classes you've taken, such as fencing classes, Shakespeare training, foreign language abilities, etc. Other things to note under special skills or hobbies are extra abilities that may be unique attributes that casting directors might seek, such as being CPR certified, a trained dancer (and which types of dance!), proficient with a musical instrument, fluent in sign language, a professional dog trainer, etc. These sections will give the casting directors a glimpse of your life outside the industry—and how well you've trained for it!

Attaching It to a Headshot

You must remember to always have your resumé stapled to the back of your headshot, back to back. In other words, when you turn the paper over, you're either looking at a headshot or resumé. Put one staple at the top and one staple at the bottom, both centered. Cut your resumé down to fit your headshot's measurements. It's never okay to paperclip your resumé to a photo, not trim the margins, or only use one staple. Be smart! Follow this simple format—it will make you appear more professional and experienced.

The Time I Failed At…

I had the opportunity to read a scene for a VP of 20th Century Fox at a national showcase I attended (I talk more about showcases in chapter five). The read went really well, so he gave me his address and asked me to send him my headshot and resumé. I was so completely thrilled that I started putting my envelope together the moment I got home:

Outdated headshot that shows me thirty pounds heavier than when he met me? Check.

Black and white headshot (when everyone in LA knows to use color headshots)? Check.

Resumé attached with one staple in the corner, like I'm turning in a school paper? Check.

Headshot measuring 8x10 while my 8.5x11 resumé flops around from behind it? Check.

Major Failure? Check.

Did I ever hear back from him? Shut up. Of course I didn't. Know who you are sending your headshot to. Are they in LA? Then it needs to be in color. Make sure your headshot looks like the same person they just met. Staple your resumé back to back. And, for goodness sakes, trim your resumé to an 8x10 size so that it matches your headshot.

Chapter Four
Making a Reel

A reel is your virtual resumé. It should show a variety of quality projects you've done, along with your name and contact information. A director, agent, or manager can look at your headshot and resumé and tell if you're handsome or if you've been cast before, but not necessarily if you can act. The reel provides the key to prove your resumé is true and show that you are excellent at what you do.

A reel used to be considered an extra perk that only actors with a lot of spare cash lying around invested in. Nowadays, however, it's an absolute must for any serious actor planning to pursue film and TV. While sitting in Q&As for the dozens of casting director workshops I've taken, every single casting director has admitted that they do look at reels when an agent or manager attaches them to an electronic submission, and they do prefer that their submissions include them. If there are 100 submissions and 10 of those have reels attached, you want to be one of those 10 (the submission process is explained in detail in chapter six). If you have a reel, you will definitely be remembered better than the others who don't.

The casting director posts the breakdown online and your agent or manager recognizes which roles you would be appropriate for. When your agent or manager submits your electronic picture and resumé, they also have the option to include a reel. While looking over the hundreds of submissions on their computer screen (each headshot is seen as a thumbnail, no bigger than one inch), the casting director can tell which submissions include a reel and which ones do not.

Now riddle me this: Suppose you are able to obtain copies of the work you have done, and you know that the casting director will be comparing your photo to hundreds of other photos of people who look just like you. Wouldn't you want to use those copies of the work you've done to show them why they should call you in for the audition instead of That Other Actor Without a Reel? Correct. Of course you would. Make a reel. Make it happen.

Making a Reel in Six Easy Steps

1. Collect Footage
Gather up all the video you have of yourself acting on tape. Short films, student films, webisodes—you name it. Don't forget you can create

the footage if you don't have any footage from jobs yet.

2. Prioritize

Just like your resumé, put it in order from your biggest credit to smallest credit. The commercial you did for the local car dealer? Near the front of the pile. A webisode filmed with a friend's family camcorder? Near the end of the pile. Grandma video taping you pretending to be a monkey? Maybe skip that one altogether. For sure.

3. Keep it Concise

Take a look at what you have. Keep in mind that your reel should only be one to two minutes in length, and casting may only watch the first thirty seconds (just like when they glance at your resumé and only see the top few things in each column). Try to get an idea of which projects you should leave out (lesser quality) and which ones you are sure you would like to include (highest quality).

4. Showcase Your Skills

Now that you have your projects narrowed down in front of you (more than one, as many as six or seven), try to determine which scenes showcase some really meaty acting. Note that the point of your reel is not to tell a story. The clips you're providing are for the sole purpose of showing your acting ability, not so they can understand your scene. You're going to have to cut in and out of dialogue, but don't be concerned that there is no plotline or your lines don't make sense. They should see that you can act, and the more clips that you can showcase, the better.

5. Edit

You can choose to edit the project yourself, or you can bring these chosen scenes to a professional editor, a family member, or friend. You will need to be familiar with a video editing program like Adobe Premiere Pro, Final Cut, Windows Movie Maker, or iMovie if you're taking this on yourself. (I 'm a big fan of Premiere Pro.) Beginning with your best quality video and best performance, piece together your chosen clips, keeping the final product around two minutes. The VIP that you're sending this to does not have a lot of time in their day to watch videos. If they're only going to give you twenty seconds of their time, then make sure your best stuff is right up front.

Hint: Keep your content appropriate. Soap Opera casting directors are not the only ones who will view your reel if your agent posts it online. If you could be considered for Disney or Nickelodeon show, then you don't want to ruin your chances by turning off a family-friendly casting director with a vulgar scene.

6. Add Your Info

Have a title screen at the beginning and end of your reel with your name written in large clear letters. Some people choose to also include their phone number or their agent's phone number, but it's not a must. Make sure it stays in frame long enough for it to be read and registered in their mind—not a quick flash, but don't let it drag on either (4-5 seconds is appropriate).

Distributing Your Reel

Once you've edited your reel and figured out how to burn it to disc, make a few hard copies to keep nearby because you never know an opportunity to physically hand it off to someone will pop up. Figure out how you can package it in a professional and creative way. You want to be able to hand a casting director or producer your disc and be proud of it. This is discussed at more length in chapter eight. Uploading your reel to YouTube and emailing a link when appropriate will be the easiest and fastest way for you to share your work, but this does not cancel out the need for you to be able to hand out a physical hard copy.

Have a sleeve made or make one yourself. Many computer programs come with the ability to design a sticker made to fit DVDs or CDs. Make sure that your name, contact info, and photo are on your reel packaging. Some people include hard copy reels in agency submission envelopes, but most agents or casting directors will not look at them unless you pass the initial "I'm interested in your photo" screening. It's completely up to you and how much money and time you have to spend on mailings. Hard copy reels are handy if you do an actor's convention or monologue showcase where you know you will be meeting VIPs one-on-one and will have the opportunity to hand them your information.

Personally, I use CD cases that have a clear front and a solid black back. I use my marketing post-cards (including my name, contact info, and photo!) and fit it into the slot designed for a CD cover. I discretely secure it with glue or tape in each corner. I go the extra step to write my name and contact info on the disc itself with a perma-nent marker in case the disc and cover are ever separated. There are no rules, so find what works best for you!

Try not to miss an appropriate opportunity to hand off your reel. After all, it is basically your electronic business card! Keep some ready-to-go with your headshots in your car. If you have an Actor's Access, LA Casting, or IMDb account, you should upload your reel to your online profile. If you have your own acting website, make sure to include it there, too.

But I Don't Have Footage

When I first moved to Los Angeles, I had footage from three student films, only one of which I thought my acting was any good in. The answer to "What if I don't have footage?" is simple: get some! If you really want to be an actor, then get some. This is why it is so important to do smaller projects for free if you're not getting any auditions yet! Student films are absolutely the best way to get started on gathering video of you acting. If you have no experience under your belt, you have no business turning down projects because you think they're not big enough for you. If you try and try and still haven't booked any jobs to collect video for a reel, think about making a temporary reel with your own camera. You can always replace it later when you collect reel footage from real acting gigs.

Here's how to get started on making a reel with your *own* footage:

1. Plan out three to six scenarios that might involve a person of your type.
2. Find scenes that represent those types or write dialogue on your own. You can have someone read off-camera to you or have them act with you but plan to edit in such a way where your monologue (from a

47

larger conversation) or dialog is the majority of the scene that is used.

3. Match wardrobe for each character and brainstorm places in your area where each scene could believably take place. Use a blank wall if necessary, but aim for making your shot believable.

4. Find a camera and a patient friend who has a free weekend and a steady hand. Spend an hour or two filming each scenario.

When I first started, I created my own reel. In order to show my acting range, I included both dramatic and comedic scenes. Some actors choose to only do one or the other. It is entirely up to you. I created scenes and places to go with each type. I brainstormed character types I wanted to include:

○ A snobby mean girl threatens another (off-camera) student to plant a diary in a locker. (Film in front of high school on a Saturday) COMEDIC

○ A daughter tries to convince her dad over a meal at the dinner table that her grades are so good she should be allowed to go to prom (Film at kitchen table and eat during the scene) COMEDIC

○ A girl gets a call from a guy she thought was going to be her boyfriend, but it turns out he confesses to liking someone else. (Film on apartment balcony on the phone) DRAMATIC

o With bruises and heavy-makeup, a girl sits in an alley and asks the person confronting her to find something better to do than bother her. (Film in alley behind apartment) DRAMATIC

o A teenager prays to God and asks Him to help her through her tears (Film in laundry room corner) DRAMATIC

o A new driver tries to convince a cop not to give her a ticket (Film outside apartment in driver's seat, looking out the window to off-camera cop) COMEDIC

After I finished filming all six, I went to work editing. I determined the order of the six scenes based on which I felt were my strongest. I ended up cutting two scenarios out altogether because of length.

My point is, even if you don't have copies of your previous performances, you can still create a solid reel. Be creative and have fun. Aim for the highest quality of acting and filming possible.

People You Should Know

You can buy sleeves to hand out hard copies of your acting reel at a place like Staples or Best Buy, or you could order online in bulk here:

- *www.uline.com*
- *www.sleevetown.com*

I recommend learning how to use an editing program yourself to edit your reel, but if you don't have time or can't make it happen you can use professional editing services like these:

- *www.reelsforactors.com*
- *http://makeitreel.net*

If you're in Los Angeles and have the spare cash, you can use this company to help create scenes for a reel instead of doing it yourself:

- *www.createyourreel.com*
- *www.speedreels.com*

Chapter Five
Representation

No two performers have the same story on how they got their start. Almost every soul in LA has a different approach, a technique to the way they handle their business or they get a fluke meeting with an agent that landed them a chance role, etc. Most things in the industry can be done in different ways. That being said, don't go breaking the rules before you learn what the rules are.

It's almost impossible to be successful going solo in this town. If you really want to be a working performer, you absolutely must try to get an agent or a manager. Your representation is your team. They help fill in all the gaps in your small business that you couldn't fill in being by yourself.

I often get asked about the difference between an agent and a manager. An agent is usually the person who will procure an appointment for you (i.e. - get you in the door to audition for the casting director). A manager is usually the person who manages you as a product, such as helping you determine the correct photos, wardrobe, publicist, contract solutions, etc. I say "usually" here because everything is not black and white in this town. Sometimes managers can get appointments for their clients and sometimes agents help choose headshots. Another significant difference is that agents typically have hundreds of clients, whereas managers often only represent 10 or fewer. Typically, I speak with my manager once or twice a day, sometimes more if it's during a busy season. My agent and I speak about once a month because my agent is constantly on the computer and phone looking for and booking appointments for his clients. My manager has more time to focus on me and answer my questions. Both are essential and have a very important role in my business.

Strategies for Getting Representation

Personal Recommendations
If you're assertive about plugging into the acting community of classes, workshops, and networking groups, you're bound to run into other actors who have representation. It's not uncommon for actors to nudge each other and ask, "Would you mind giving your agent my headshot?" It happens all the time. I've been able to get some of my friends an interview before, and I've asked friends to recommend me to their agent as well. It's your job to have the resumé, photo, and acting chops to have a stellar meeting and get signed, but getting a little help to get in the door could be your ticket to representation.

I found my manager through a recommendation. I was working as a stand-in for Sam Raimi's horror film *Drag Me To Hell*, and Sam is the type of director who likes his stand-ins to actually perform the dialogue and the action. One of the principal actresses on set was watching the monitor by the director and noticed my acting chops. She pulled me aside and asked if I had a manager yet. When I told her I didn't, she said, "I know a great one you should meet!" She made a phone call for me and, a week later, I met the wonderful Michael Wallach. He has been on my team ever since!

Social Meeting

You'd be surprised how small of a town LA can be. Agents and managers are people too, right? They eat (at restaurants), they shop (at malls), and they caffeinate (at Starbucks). You meet businessmen and nannies and policemen and moms and writers out in the real world, so why not agents? Keep your resumé in your car because you never know who you're going to meet. Don't just throw it in the backseat with your McDonald's trash. Invest in a professional-looking folder to keep your headshots safe from spilled soda.

Mass Mailing

This is a very common way that actors in LA receive representation. Check out chapter eight for tips on how to work out your own personalized marketing strategy to get your name and face out there!

Showcase/Convention

Attending a showcase is the entire reason I decided to move to LA. It's also how I got my very first LA agent! I highly recommend attending conventions and showcases. I've seen more success stories happen overnight at these babies than you can imagine.

Showcases and conventions allow you to compete against your fellow performers—and be judged, ranked, and rewarded accordingly. Usually, the judges are industry guests (think: agents, managers, casting directors, producers, choreographers, or directors) looking for new talent to either represent or recommend to their industry peers. Normally these events have an entry fee of some sort, but if you've got a talent in this business, you could emerge from the event with anything from a cash prize to an interview with a manager to a taped audition with a casting director! Who knows?

A few years ago, I attended a showcase that was started by a woman named Millie Lewis. Her daughter, Carey Arban, now leads the convention, and it is her desire to run a family-friendly event where actors, models, singers, and dancers can pursue the industry in a safe and nurturing environment. The whole event is focused on talent and faith, and growing, merging, and balancing the two. I cannot express to you what an amazing opportunity this was! Can you even imagine being able to practice, pursue, fail, get back up, and learn in an environment that is coated with people of morals and family values? Unbelievable.

I heard about the audition for my first convention on the radio while I was driving around in my rattling pick-up truck in my hometown of Omaha, Nebraska:

"Do you want to be a STAR?" station 104.5 asked as I sat in my pick-up truck at the longest red light in the world.

"Why, yes! Yes, 104.5, I do want to be a star!" I stared at my dashboard, waiting for more.

"Then come on down to our open auditions and give it a shot!"

So I did. I attended the open call and arrived with a prepared monologue I had memorized for a speech class in school. A national talent scout named Kim Myers patiently watched everyone— and I mean everyone. Seriously, you would not believe the kinds of people who show up wanting to, um, shake what their mama's gave 'em! I listened to Kim explain the event and the types of people who had been discovered by attending and competing. I knew that waiting around in Nebraska for an agent to "discover" me was highly unlikely; I had to be proactive! I am so grateful that Kim saw something in me—that single audition changed my life. After I received a callback from her and an invitation to attend, I knew I needed to say yes.

This particular showcase takes place in Orlando, once in the summer and once in the winter. You can compete in a number of events like Monologue, Cold Read, Singing, Dancing, Commercial, Scene Study, Fashion Runway, etc. You compete against other contestants who are invited to attend the event from all over the country, plus a few from countries like Portugal and Scotland. The cool thing about conventions like these is that the judges for each event are VIPs in the industry, and you have a front-row ticket to perform in front of them! The more events you compete in, the more these VIPs will see you on stage.

When I say "VIPs," I'm talking about top professionals in the industry. Managers, agents, casting directors, and producers from New York and LA and Chicago and Atlanta, who you wouldn't be able to meet one-on-one with in their offices in a million years! Of course, they'll see you perform when you compete in your event, but you'll also get a chance to talk to them face-to-face on Interview Day. This is an open time where you can meet each industry professional and "sell yourself" in a speed-interview style. There is also a chance to speak with VIPs if (or when!) they give you a callback.

I poured my heart and soul into preparing to go to Orlando. I memorized all my lines, carefully chose my wardrobe, read acting books, took workshops, and really went the extra mile to make sure I could be as prepared as possible for my competitions. I saved up money for six months and paid for the entire thing myself. I carpooled with four others and sat cross-legged on an ice chest for the entire road trip. In the ice chest? The PB&J I brought to eat all week. I wanted to make this trip happen and I did whatever it took to get there.

By the time I arrived at the convention, I was totally ready and competed in six events. My hard work paid off—I was rewarded on the last day with callbacks. Each was from a different VIP (a casting director from New York, an agent from LA, the VP of casting for 20th Century Fox, etc.). The callbacks were essentially a private interview time where these industry professionals could let me know if they were interested in signing me. I had so many opportunities to choose from, and I felt that the time, money, and energy I put into the event had really paid off. I chose an agency offer in LA and moved there the following summer.

If you're already in a big city like Chicago or LA, there are local showcases you can attend for one night at a time, as opposed to a weeklong event where you travel to another location. Some acting workshops and companies will host an Agent's Night where they bring in a guest agent who is looking to bring in more clients. They could invite you to perform a monologue and charge an entry fee for you to be seen and judged. The experience and confidence you gain by participating in this kind of showcase is invaluable, not to mention the possibility of a contract!

People You Should Know

These showcases put you in front of top agents, managers, and casting directors from across the country:

- o *www.amtcworld.com*
- o *www.theartstalent.com*

I take workshops in LA with a company called Act Now, which mostly host casting director classes but occasionally do have an agent night. Check them out (ask for my consultant, Michelle!) *Website: www.actnownetwork.com*

I also have found a workshop site called The Actors Key to be very helpful. These workshops are super cheap (about 30 bucks) and they are one-on-one style, where it's just you and the casting director in the room. The cool thing about this place is that they love to bring agents and mangers in, and these workshops are only 10 bucks! Because it's one-on-one in the room (just you and the agent), you can bring in your own scene instead of cold reading with a partner. www.actorskey.com

Chapter Six

Auditions

When I first moved to LA, I had only auditioned for one real film and a few theatre productions. Now that I know a little bit more, I'm embarrassed to think of what a fool I made of myself during those first three or four tries out here in the real world! Let me do you a favor and share with you some of the basics, so you don't audition wearing a giant sign that reads, "Hey, everybody! Look at me! I'm a total rookie!"

Auditions are the key to getting acting work. Period. 99 percent of the time you can't get a role unless you audition—and that rare one percent are people like Brad Pitt or Tom Cruise who are in high demand, though even they must sometimes audition for highly competitive roles.

How to Get an Audition

With Representation

Most auditions are scored through an agent or a manager. If you are new to acting and don't have representation yet, there are also a few ways to score auditions on your own.

Your agent will be the primary way you *get legitimate* auditions. In other words, if you were to book the job, you would actually get paid a legitimate amount of money. Managers can occasionally get an audition for you, but most often that is not their primary role. In LA, there are two major casting websites your agent or manger will use that any serious actor should know about: Breakdown Services and LA Casting.

Breakdownservices.com (also simply called "Breakdowns") is the online forum for casting directors to post what roles they're looking for. Only agents and managers have access to this website. This site is how the majority of film and TV shows are cast. Let's use it in a sentence: "Hey, can you check Breakdowns to see if there is a role for me in that project?"

"Breakdowns" also has another common meaning. It is also a term for the specific roles and character descriptions needed for any project (film, modeling, theatre, etc.) It is where a casting director will "break down" what is needed for each character, such as body type, age, gender, etc. For example: "Can you send me the (character) breakdown so I can decide what I should wear to my audition?"

To summarize, your representation will find breakdowns on Breakdowns. Make sense?

Let's get back to the only breakdowns *you* need to worry about. A character's breakdown is the information that you will use to prepare for your audition: age, personality, gender, wardrobe notes, etc. Here are a few examples of breakdowns for a film. These are the sorts of breakdowns your representation will find on Breakdowns. (Confused yet?)

[Jenna Bronson] 14 - 15. Attractive, smart aleck, and too cool for school, Jenna can't stand the members of her own family. She doesn't understand why her father insists on treating her Grandma like a princess and would rather hole up with a video game in her room than speak to anyone human. All was well in the world of teenage denial until her Grandma's health begins to fail and Jenna finds herself on a journey of self-discovery... LEAD. SUBMIT ALL ETHNICITIES. MINORS: PLEASE NOTE AGE ON SUBMISSIONS

[Mr. Bronson] In his 40s, a wealthy investor, Mr. Bronson has had so much success in the stock market that he doesn't have to work anymore. He is Jenna's father and lives with her in Springfield, Missouri. Mr. Bronson is a single dad and counts on the wisdom of his mother, Grandma, to help parent through Jenna's teen years. Mr. Bronson doesn't notice that Grandma's advice rarely makes sense... SUPPORTING. SUBMIT ALL ETHNICITIES

[GRANDMA]   A jaded and angry   70-year-old woman, she is the mother of Mr. Bronson and the grandmother of Jenna. She is physically and mentally debilitated and often breaks out into song unexpectedly. When her health begins to fail and Grandma realizes she is nearing the end, love for her child and grandchild fights its   way   to   the surface of her unstable personality... SUPPORTING. SUBMIT ALL ETHNICITIES

In this scenario, the casting director is looking for three people for this upcoming film. The breakdown will also list the production's start dates and location. When an agent logs into their Breakdown account online, they can see daily updates of all roles being cast. The agent will compare the character descriptions to their agency's personal inventory of actors, then submit an electronic version of actors' headshots and resumés. Perhaps the agent has five 14-year-olds that could pull off the snotty character of Jenna, three 40-somethings that really play "Dad" well, and one 60-year-old that always books elderly roles. The agent will then submit the information for his clients, and then wait to see if the casting director responds.

The casting director or casting director's assistant will be checking on Breakdowns for the agency submissions that come in throughout the day. As they see headshots and resumés that (hopefully) match what they are looking for, the casting director will sort through them to determine which actors they'd like to see in person. They'll choose based on which headshots stand out to them, which agency names are respected and reputable, which resumés impress them, which actor names they recognize, which reel catches their eye, etc. One actor I met once said he was called in because the casting director thought his name was funny.

The casting office will then contact the selected actors' agent. In this scenario, maybe the Grandma submission and two of the Jenna submissions met their approval. The office assigns a specific audition time to each actor and notifies the actor's representation, who in turn notifies the actor. As the actor, if you receive a voicemail or email with the audition details, it is imperative that you let your agent know you received the information. This is an important professional step that will keep your representation happy and you on-time to auditions.

Without Representation

Remember, you can get auditions on your own if you don't have an agent yet. You absolutely must sign up at www.actorsaccess.com and put your current headshots and resumés on your account. Actorsaccess.com is basically Breakdowns that actors have access to. After browsing through the daily breakdowns, you can pay a submission fee for auditions you feel match your type, which we discussed in chapter two. (Note: an agent or manager will not have to pay for each submission. The fee only applies if you as an actor are submitting yourself.)

Checking craiglist.com, backstagewest.com, lacasting.com, and meeting casting directors through workshops are also great ways to get auditions. A casting director can call you directly for an audition if you've provided your cell phone number or personal email on your resumé, but this is rare. Remember, you're only auditioning on your own until you get representation to pursue it for you. Theatre in LA rarely pays well enough to tempt your agent to pursue that work for you. If you want to audition at a theatre in LA to build your experience and resumé, you'll most likely have to pursue those opportunities on your own.

Preparing for an Audition
Auditions are essentially job interviews, so make sure your appearance, punctuality, and professionalism are no different than they would be for a big job interview.

You can get a call for an audition anywhere from a week before you're seen or as late as 30 minutes beforehand—another reason it is important to have a flexible survival job and ready-to-go headshots in your car! A call about an audition will include basic information about the audition's location, time, etc.

Never, ever, ever underestimate LA traffic. Google Map every step of the way if you're going into unfamiliar territory. In the good old days (pre-2010, when I got my first smartphone), it wasn't uncommon for me to call my best friend at her computer across the country and ask her to look up an address for me because I was turned around and was running late. Using that GPS in your phone is of course a great idea—but we all know they can occasionally be wrong so be sure to still map out your route ahead of time.

You'll be given a specific appointment time for many auditions. Be sure to arrive early! For commercials, it is common to have a time frame as opposed to one specific appointment time. For example, they might be seeing a specific character, like "young African American dads," from 1-4 p.m. This helps a ton when you're facing traffic and trying to switch your survival job shift around. Make sure you get the correct time frame because you don't want to show up when they're at lunch or after your character's frame has ended.

Don't forget to leave time for parking. Sometimes the answer is a parking garage and sometimes there is only metered parking available. You'll need to keep your ashtray stocked with quarters. I've almost missed auditions on more than one occasion because audition parking lots can be quite complicated and crowded. Try to anticipate what you're driving into before you get there.

What to Expect at the Audition

Video Recording

Almost every audition I've been to in LA has a camera running somewhere in the room. This is either for the casting directors to refresh themselves on a particular performance later, to reference for future projects, or to show to the decision-makers (producers, director, etc.) after the auditions are over.

Slate

This is the 5-15 second introduction you'll make at the start of the audition where you look directly into the camera and state your name clearly. Sometimes they'll ask you to "slate" your name and height or name and agency or name as you turn profile so they can see what you look like from the side, etc. Sometimes the decision maker will be screening a lengthy audition tape, skipping through every audition and only watching the slates. When they see someone they think they like, they continue playing the tape and only then will watch that person's performance. Frustrating, but true.

One strategy for slates is to do them in character and make them as long as possible. For example, if a man is auditioning for a scary axe-murderer (just like his mother always dreamed for him!), he might "slate" with a low, menacing voice, "Good afternoon, my name is Mark Taylor and I'm auditioning for the role of Scary Axe Murderer." Instead of just saying his name for only two seconds, the actor took three times that long. In theory, if this particular director or producer were fast-forwarding through slates, the actor would get more screen time to be considered than his fellow actors. I occasionally do this, depending on the role, but I find that most decision makers will see you in person at the callback anyway. I choose to focus on my dialogue and making the scene excellent, as opposed to stressing about how many seconds long my slate is. It's your choice!

Mark

This is literally a mark on the floor—a piece of tape in the shape of a "T" or an "X" on the floor in front of the casting table and camera. If they ask you to "hit the mark" or "find your mark" at a certain time, that means you need to land there with your feet on the tape. Sounds simple, right? Well, try not knowing what a mark is. (Been there.)

MARK!

Commercial Auditions

Commercials can definitely be a cash cow for many actors. There are local commercials that air in your surrounding city or state, and there are national commercial jobs that could pay you enough for your children's college education!

Commercial spots can be funny (think Super Bowl) or extremely serious (Public Service Announcements, or PSAs). If the commercials are run locally or on the web, it's possible you could be paid for the day's work and given a copy the next week. National spots could pay you a "buy out" fee of, oh, $100,000, or pay you every single time the commercial airs for all the years to follow! If you're lucky enough to get an audition for a commercial, don't scoff because they're asking you to pretend that you like chicken. Dance your chicken-heart out and it could buy you a new house.

Casting directors will post commercial breakdowns on a special page within a website called lacasting.com (or commercial postings sometimes land on breakdowns or castingfrontier.com) that only agents and managers can see. There are some general submissions open to everyone on these sites for people who are not represented by an agent or manager. Some commercials that are casting extras or background actors will advertise on craigslist.com.

Here are some examples of commercial audition notices:

McDonald's (national SAG commercial)
Date: Monday
Time: 11:55 a.m.

Timeframe: 10:30 a.m. - 1:30 p.m.
Location: Ocean Park Casting 27 PARK BLVD
Attire: red polo shirt, khakis
Role Name: Female crew member (white)
Role Details: Female, white, 16-20 years. Average looks, interesting faces, not overly quirky or character-y.

Verisign, an Internet securities company (national SAG commercial)
Date: Tomorrow
Time: 3:00 p.m.
Time Frame: This is a callback. Arrive at 3 p.m.
Location: The Casting Lounge 1035 La Brea Ave
Attire: Nice Casual
Role Name: Teen Student Driver
Role Details: 18 to look younger. Juno-ish type guys and girls. Can have braces and pigtails, but not necessary. Boys can be like a young Michael Cera and other real, believable teenage boy looks.
Note: Bring two headshots, resumés, and bar-codes.

Wendy's (national SAG commercial)
Date: Friday
Time: 4:10 p.m.
Time Frame: 3:30-5:00 p.m.
Location: Ocean Park Casting 27 PARK BLVD
Attire: black pants/green, blue, orange polo shirt
Role Name: male crew member

Role Details: Male, Caucasian, 32-42 years.
Looking for an excellent actor with strong comedy/improv background. Talent should be unique in their own affable, likeable way. Honest and real. They should convey a genuine enthusiasm for what they do and where they work. Normal looking; not model-y.
Notes: Street parking recommended as there is a fee for parking garage.

Most commercial casting directors don't even take a headshot these days (bring one anyway); some prefer electronic copies—this is where the barcode comes in. There is database for casting directors called The Casting Frontier that sets up a commercial profile for you, including posting your resumé and headshots online. For these auditions, you do not have to waste a headshot; instead, simply have your barcode and bring it with you. Maybe someone has told you that in Hollywood, you're only a number to people. Wrong! It's a barcode. So, actually, you're more like a product.

Your agency will always tell you what role you're going to be auditioning for. Most likely, that character/role will come with a description of either a few words or sentences, like wardrobe notes. If they say to wear a white dress, then for heaven's sake, wear a white dress. If they say "a tie-wearing businessman with a cell phone," then put on a tie and bring your cell phone with you. It's not rocket science. Oh, but turn your phone off.

When you arrive at the commercial casting office, you'll notice that it is quite different from film, TV, and theatre spaces. Usually the common areas are huge and have up to ten private audition rooms. Each room usually has a bulletin board or small table outside the door. By looking at each board, you'll see which commercials are being held where, and you'll be able to sign up for a time to be seen. Even if your appointment was at 3:15, if you sign up at 2:30 and no one else is waiting, they'll bring you in.

On the board, you could find a number of things:

- o Storyboards
- o A summary of the story
- o Copies of the script for you to memorize
- o Directions for when you're in the room

Most commercial casting directors like to take groups of actors in together to explain the scenario to everyone at once. They then release you back to the lobby, calling in one name at a time to record the audition. You'll find each office and casting director works a bit differently, but most auditions are run the same way.

Types of Commercial Auditions

Auditions for commercials are some of the most interesting and fun appointments you'll ever have! Most of the time you never know what you're going to be doing before you get there, and that's part of what makes them so different. They could be improv, a photo, or reading a scene—it's a grab bag!

Individual Scene

I once auditioned for a cable company commercial. My role as "Girl" came with no wardrobe notes. The character description simply read "hilarious and awful singer." I arrived at my audition and checked the bulletin board. They had tacked up a full script of the commercial, and my part involved thinking that I'm going to be the next American Idol while singing horribly in the street as people walk by. There is absolutely no way to prepare for that! When they called my name, I went into the room and the guy taping the auditions explained that I was supposed to hold the guitar and—

"But I don't know how to play the guitar," I interrupted.

"Even better," he smiled.

On "action," my job was to sing anything and pretend that I was amazing. Easy as pie.

Sometimes, when you arrive at the office and notice that your scene involves more than just you, that means they will pair you up with another actor to read opposite your role or the casting director/assistant will read lines with you off-camera. If you are able to, memorizing the lines is the best way to go. Most often, the dialogue will be written for you on a big script inside the room, but the more you can look directly into the camera or at your scene partner, the better. This is when audition practice really pays off.

Improv

I auditioned for a Coca-Cola commercial once where they told me I would be seen for the part of a cute cheerleader. I dressed my cutest (not in a full uniform, although some girls there did have theirs on!) and showed up with a high ponytail and lots of glitter. I signed in and was called in for a group explanation. The casting assistant explained that we would be seen in groups of six. As a group, we should stay in character and talk as if we were leaving a football game in the 1960's. So I went in with two other cheerleaders and three football players, and we chatted for about four minutes about the big game and the upcoming spring dance. Be prepared to make up dialog on the spot!

Photo

I auditioned for a Nike commercial once where the role read "Young female athlete" and the wardrobe notes read, "young, athletic, and trendy look."

I walked into the casting office and found the bulletin board completely blank. The assistant walked out, asked if I was here for Nike, and showed me where to sign in.

Then she said, "I'm just going to take your Polaroid."

Easy. As. Pie. But try not to remember this story when you're plugging a parking meter with quarters and wondering how many more to add. Add them.

The Coveted Callback: Commercials

Usually the casting director or casting assistant will have seen you for the first round of auditions, but don't be surprised if there are a few extra people in the room for the callback. I've been in callback rooms where there have been almost twenty people watching from behind the camera! The people that represent the company/product, the ad agency, and the commercial's director, will most likely be in the room.

Film/TV Auditions

Preparing for Film/TV Auditions

The information you'll receive when you get your audition notice for both film and TV are basically the same: time, date, address, and role. Most likely your agent will attach the break-down. There will always be sides (your lines) attached to the emailed audition notice or available to download online. Whether or not you want to memorize your lines is solely your choice, but I find that the higher the stakes are, the more certain I want to be of my lines.

Once you begin auditioning on a regular basis, you'll realize that auditions for film and TV do not follow a standard format. Casting directors really differ in how they run their offices and in what they prefer from their actors. You can ask 100 different casting directors their opinion on auditions and get 100 different answers. Hopefully my advice in this section will cover most of the types of people and offices you'll come across.

You can be informed that you have an audition for TV or film anywhere from one month before the audition to one hour before. (Did I mention you should leave extra headshots in your car?) My friend once submitted himself for a role in a Civil War movie, and he got a call almost seven months later for an audition that would take place in 12 days. You really never know. I would say a "normal" heads-up for an audition would be about 1-3 days notice.

The typical audition notice will be given to you by your agent, manager, or from the casting office directly if you don't have representation. They will tell you what time, what role, and provide you with the dialogue. Once you have your audition details (location, character, and script/sides), you should become as familiar as you can with the material.

Here is where one of those big discrepancies comes in. I've been told by casting directors that you shouldn't memorize because it gives the impression that you're presenting your finished product and you're not going to get any better after that. I've also been told that you should always memorize your lines (if you have time) so you can be free from the pages in your hand and look up towards your reader or scene partner. I tend to lean towards the second opinion, because, in my mind, I want to seem capable of learning dialogue and be super comfortable not looking down at the pages. But I also understand the need to project that I have room to learn and grow. I do this by being very flexible in the casting room, willing to switch my interpretation on a dime if the casting director suggests I read it another way.

Even if the director or casting director's suggestion is the stupidest thing you have ever heard, you should pretend that it is a great idea and be absolutely willing to try to read your scene that way. This could be the difference between landing a role and being dismissed because you appear rude. Nod and smile immediately and appear willing and able, even if the idea seems intimidating. Everyone likes people who like their ideas. And you want the director to like you.

Types of Film Auditions

Feature Films
You will get major feature film auditions solely through your agent or manager. It is extremely rare that you will be able to submit for a role on your own, without representation. Sometimes there are exceptions posted on actorsaccess.com when casting directors are seeking something specific and difficult to find, such as a young

Jennifer Lopez between the ages of four and seven who can also juggle fireballs.

Some casting directors have a cozy, permanent office. Others are in a temporary set-up with blank walls. Some have the comforts of a successful sitcom paying their bills while others are renting out office space in a crowded downtown building. Either way, the staff will most certainly be professional and the stakes are definitely raised from that non-Equity theatre audition you had a week ago. If you're in a casting lobby, waiting to be seen for a part in a feature film (one line or one billion lines), then congratulations are in order! You've reached a point in your career that thousands have never accomplished.

Feature film audition breakdowns will usually provide you with the director and producer names, along with the name of the studio that is backing it and any actors who are already attached to the project. I always memorize the dialogue provided to me for feature films if I have enough time because the stakes are very high at this point. Being cast in a feature film could certainly change your career (and pocketbook) overnight.

Indie Films

The majority of auditions you'll find on actor websites like craigslist.com, actorsaccess.com,

and backstagewest.com for non-represented actors are independent films. Because you're not
guaranteed money up front or at all, most agents
do not bother submitting their clients for these
types of projects. Of course, there are some indie
films that are quite promising and have a decent
budget, so you may receive auditions through
your agent in those cases.

You'll have the strangest experiences of your life
in auditions for independent films in just the
waiting room alone. When someone calls their
film "independent," it means that they don't have
financing from a major studio. So, this could be
Uncle Bob who decided to leave rebuilding junk
cars for the film industry. His filming location?
Grandma's attic. Or, it could be some fantastic
artists who really know their stuff and plan on
debuting the film at the famous Sundance Film
Festival and making millions of dollars (for example: Little Miss Sunshine, The Blair Witch Project, The Usual Suspects, Garden State, etc). Don't
automatically discount the opportunity just because the audition type says "independent."

That being said, be prepared for an unprepared
casting director. And by "casting director," I
mean the person who signs you in, calls you in,
and presses record on the camera. That person
may also be the director, writer, producer, and
actor alongside you in the film. Don't be sur-

prised if there is only one person there and this project is their baby. Expect it. And don't insult people's babies.

Student Films

Talk about a good learning experience! Working on a student film is one of the safest places you can be. (Not literally, of course, because the lighting technician doesn't know what he is doing and could possibly start a fire.) Most students in the Los Angeles area will post their auditions on craigslist.com, actorsaccess.com, or lacasting.com. There is no better place for you to learn how to behave on camera, learn what is expected of you, and make mistakes without bringing down a multi-million dollar production.

I absolutely recommend you audition for and accept roles in these types of films. Mass audiences will not see the end result so you can feel comfortable trying out different techniques, learning how to hit your mark, and holding your body under the lighting. Get your feet wet memorizing dialogue and doing a scene where you have to scream or cry on command—over and over again. The more practice you get on a simulated movie set, the more prepared you will be when you step on set for a feature film.

Warning about student films: Make sure that you get a copy of your work. It is common for a student film to say they will provide you with "copy, credit, and meals" in exchange for your work on set. (That means you're promised a copy of your work, your name in the credits, and food while you're on set.) Never expect to be paid and absolutely never pay to participate in the film. There are a number of websites you can go to print out a form that you can ask the director and producers to sign that will guarantee you get a copy of your work. Clips from movies like these are an essential part of building up your reel, and most actors do not pursue the producer or director if the DVD doesn't magically appear in the mail when promised. Do the work and be assertive. Assume they will not give you a copy on their own; get their contact information and bug them until they mail it. You did the work, so you deserve your payment. I have included a website in the "People You Should Know" section where you can find a contract you can have signed to help ensure you get your film copy and credit from student film or indy film producers.

TV Series Auditions

SAG/AFTRA shows (union shows) are posted on the online breakdowns that agents and managers have access to. On rare occasions, if they're looking for something unique, you may find a public casting call on Craigslist.com, Actorsaccess.com, or Lacasting.com. (I have mentioned those once or twice, yes?)

When you walk into the casting office of a TV series for the first time, you'll notice the difference between these spaces and commercial casting rooms right away. They're homier and personalized. The staff has been there for a number of months or years—or, in the case of some soap operas, decades! There are usually comfy couches to wait on and photos of the cast on the wall. It can be intimidating at first, but don't let that override the satisfaction you should feel for sitting in a legit casting office.

If the show has gone past the initial pilot stages, chances are they have a system down for casting. If you are called in more than once, you'll get to know the casting assistant who usually has a desk in the waiting area for actors. The sign-in sheet will always be in the same place, and you'll learn the best places to park and the quickest way to walk through the studio lot to get to the audition room.

If you are called in for a TV show, you know that the casting director recognizes that you are a right fit for the series. Almost all casting directors save the headshots of promising performers who are right for the show, so don't panic if you don't book a role on your first or second call to the office. For example, I am blonde, quirky, and look young, so my "look" is right for comedies or dramas that feature older teens. If I have a good read at a first audition, I keep in touch through postcards and know I'll most likely be back in again. (I auditioned twice for small co-star roles on *90210* before finally auditioning for and booking a recurring guest star role: Cousin Emily.)

The Coveted Callback: Film/TV

Your first audition, called a pre-read, will most likely be with the casting director only, often just an assistant (not the head casting director—the the big boss!), to sift through the masses and find a select few for the callback. Directors and producers rarely attend a pre-read, as it is a waste of their valuable time. There can be 50-200 actors brought in for a pre-read! Pre-reads are almost always recorded via a videocamera in the room, especially if an assistant is doing the screening instead of a head casting director. That tape can be used to directly cast the role (that happened to me for my roles on American Horror Story and Suburgatory), but often you'll have a callback before booking the role.

At a callback, definitely count on the head casting director being present in the room, as well as the director for the film or television episode. There will often be at least one producer in the room and sometimes the writer as well. Callbacks can have anywhere from two to as many as 20 actors in attendance.

If your callback goes well, you may be invited to attend a producer session. This works the same way as a callback, but more important people are in the room and the number of actors they are considering has gone way down. Sometimes the head of the network will be in the room, along with executive producers. These are the auditions you dream about having! Whether you land the role or not, a lot of important people have seen you and—hopefully!—will remember you for next time.

If you knock their socks off at a producer session, you may be invited to do a screen test with the other actors in the series. You'll only go this far in the process if this role is really important, such as the lead in a new series, a new recurring character on a show, etc. They may put you in makeup and wardrobe for this or take you to a set with props, but don't expect that. Each show has their own way of doing things.

Theatre Auditions

Actors' Equity Association (AEA) is the theatre union for actors. Being a member of the union (called "being Equity") is one of the only ways that you can be paid to act in theatre. New York City is by far the best place to be if you want to be auditioning constantly for Equity shows, but other major cities (Chicago, LA, etc.) can provide work for AEA members as well. Fortunately, even if you're non-Equity, there are a few ways to be seen in the audition room for Equity auditions, called Equity Principal Auditions (EPAs).

Most theatre productions in LA are non-Equity. A production is only considered Equity if they are working with AEA and agree to their rules and employ people who are a part of that association (including cast and crew). There is a point system that must be followed to join the union, which I will explain later.

Getting a Theatre Audition

Union (Equity) auditions are posted on Breakdowns for agents. You can, however, see a limited amount of the audition listings agents see by checking out actorsaccess.com. Remember, it is okay to check out actors access and go to auditions for theatre even when you have representation; your manager and agent usually won't mind you getting these auditions on your own.

Non-union auditions are posted on those three magical websites I keep mentioning. You're more likely to get an audition for non-union theatre by checking audition dates on individual theatre company websites or backstagewest.com than waiting for a call from your representation. Agents in LA rarely get you auditions for non-union theatre projects because they pay very little, if at all.

Preparing for a Theatre Audition

Once you know what play and character you're going to read for, make sure you understand what the director wants you to do when you're at the audition. More often than not, you'll be reading pieces from the play with another actor auditioning or with a designated reader who is working with the theatre. Occasionally, the director or theater will ask all auditioning actors to come prepared with a monologue and not read from the play itself at all. If this is the case, make sure you find a monologue portraying a character that is similar to the role you'd like to be cast in. There is no point in reading a monologue that portrays a nasty villain if your goal is to be the humble young prince, right?

If you have a few days to get ready, do your best to memorize the lines from the scene. If you're notified about the audition several days in advance, you must have the scene(s) memorized. Hold the pages of the scene in your hand during the audition just in case you have a momentary lapse.

Try your best to work through some physical possibilities for your character: how they'd hold themselves, how they'd walk, when they'd sit down, etc. Anything that can give your character movement during your audition will help you appear more comfortable and like a veteran of the stage. Think about what your character would wear and begin to put pieces from your closet together. If the play is a period piece, I recommend women wear skirts and heels and men wear dress shoes. You do move differently when dressed appropriately, and I think it makes a big difference in your believability on stage. Would you cast an Ebenezer Scrooge who came to the audition in flip-flops and cargo shorts?

If you only have a few hours' notice, get as familiar with the audition piece as you can in the time that you have. Either way, memorized or not, you should be holding the pages from the scene in your hand. Do as much as you can to be able to look at the person you're speaking with. Just like your acting teacher told you, don't look down at your script or hands for entire lines at a time.

At Non-Union Theatre Auditions

When you audition for a play, you'll almost always know what show you're auditioning for beforehand. Maybe the theatre has posted it on their website, maybe you read about it in a newspaper (wait, does that still happen?!), or maybe you heard about it from a friend. In any case, you should know the name of the show you're reading for or at least their shows for the upcoming season. For the responsible actor, it's important to find a copy of the show and read it completely. That way, you'll know which role is right for you. On a rare occasion, I've auditioned for shows that are brand new, so I ask the person who is setting up the audition for a list of characters and a summary/plot synopsis. This is an important part of preparing your audition!

When you get to the theater, sometimes they'll have a sign-up sheet and sometimes they won't.

If they do, they'll most likely ask you what character you're planning to audition for, your name, contact info, and perhaps what agency you're coming from. You should bring a headshot with your resumé stapled to the back (back-to-back).

There is usually a lobby of some sort for you to wait in. Try not to get too caught up in analyzing the other people in the room. Reread your lines, take a deep breath, and—just like Mama taught you—make sure you don't have to go to the bathroom. Mentally prepare yourself for anything in the room—the director could decide they want you to deliver your monologue sitting down with no movement at all or standing on your head. (I'm sure it has happened to someone. Maybe.) Don't be thrown off if they give you limitations that will keep you from doing the scene how you rehearsed it. Don't expect to read on a stage or with props. The more flexible you can be going into the audition room, the better it will go, in regard to your nerves and your audition as a whole.

At Union Auditions
If you are non-Equity and auditioning for a union show, you should plan to arrive early. There's no exact science to it. For shows like Wicked, actors have been known to show up five hours before

the monitor arrives. For a little-known theater casting a new show no one has heard of before, you could be ten minutes early and be just fine. Use your good judgment.

At an Equity audition, a monitor is the person helping to run the auditions. He or she is the person to see about signing in and getting any questions answered that you may have. The monitor usually gets to the audition 30-60 minutes before it begins.

If the monitor is not there when you arrive, you can hop in line or be the first to get one going. When the monitor shows up, he or she will let you sign in on the non-union sheet and most likely tell you a time to check back in with him or her. At that time, he or she will have a better idea of whether or not the director will see any non-union actors at the auditions.

There are typically four sign-in lists at most Equity auditions. Sign-in sheet priority goes like this:

1. All Equity actors will sign in according to the order that they arrive, or their names will already be listed next to their scheduled appointment time. (If you are Equity, sometimes you can schedule an audition at a specific time.)

2. If there are more Equity actors than there are spaces, a sign-in sheet called the Alternate List will begin to fill up. If anyone were to cancel their audition, miss his or her name being called, or if auditions are running ahead of schedule, the monitor will begin to call in these Equity actors from the overflow Alternate List because they have second priority.

3. The third sign-in sheet is for Equity Membership Candidates. These non-Equity actors have acquired points towards his or her Equity card by having been previously cast in an Equity show or having worked at an Equity theatre. These actors will be seen if all Equity overflow actors have been seen.

4. The fourth and final list is for the non-Equity actors with no points. Some directors will tell the monitor beforehand that they waive their right to see non-Equity actors and the sheet will be tossed. You would, however, be able to leave a headshot and resumé for consideration. Even if the director does say he or she will see some non-Equity hopefuls, it doesn't guarantee they will get through the entire list.

If you are a non-Equity actor and decide to give an Equity audition a shot, I encourage you to be very patient and bring something with you to fill the time as you wait. Keep in mind that you might be waiting a long time, and it's not wise to step outside for a phone call or smoke break because you might miss the monitor calling your name. If you bring work with you, it is not a waste of time. Do something productive that will benefit your career like:

- o Read an acting book
- o Use your smartphone to read updates on the latest acting blogs
- o Flip through several monologue books to look for new material
- o Bring postcards with you to write "thank you" or "checking in" notes to casting directors

These are just some suggestions, but you get the idea. Don't waste your time—force yourself to fill it. Plus, if you're called in the room, you've added a great audition to a productive waiting experience. Bravo!

The Coveted Callback: Theatre

At a callback, expect to read with other actors. The director will almost always be in the room, but it is possible that the producers or writer could be there as well. Seeing you physically next to the other performers is a big part of the casting process. Don't let them intimidate you—you were called back for a reason! Someone saw something they liked, and that's why you have every right to be proud to be there.

Prepare Yourself

Look for monologue websites or books by browsing on Google or Amazon.com. There are so many to choose from. The only hard thing about picking one is deciding which, out of hundreds, is the lucky book for you. I've found several great monologues in contemporary poetry books like *Aloud! Voices from the Nuyorican Poet's Café.* You'll be amazed at what treasures you'll find in a used bookstore. Even using pieces from a funny blog that you follow could work. An exceptional monologue website for a Shakespeare piece is www.shakespeare-monologues.org. Avoid taking monologues from famous movies. Why in the world would you want the director to compare your performance to Ian McKellen from *Lord of the Rings*? Save the "you shall not pass" speech for your shower and find something they haven't heard before.

Attend showcases and write down what monologues are given. If the actors does not say the title and author, ask the performer after he or she has finished where he or she found the piece.

Even if you can't remember it word for word, jot down moments or lines that were really funny and you can put together your own version of it. Taking things from performances you've seen that have worked (barring famous moments from movies) is a great idea. There are no copyright issues and it's not considered taboo to use this method. You're not selling it and calling it your own, right? (Your answer better be "right!") Just use it as a monologue and be honest about how you found it if you're asked.

Keep a record of your auditions. Write down the audition details, especially the casting director's name and address.

And *please* keep extra shoes and headshots in your car!

What You Can Do Right Now

o Start getting a monologue inventory together with a variety of different characters you could play

o Look on your local city's Craigslist page under "Gigs" for "Talent" opportunities, such as local shows, modeling, commercials, etc. Attend as many of these auditions as you can to make your TV/film resumé that much bigger when you move to the city. Even if you don't land anything, think of all that audition experience you'll have under your belt.

o Call local theaters or check out their websites to see if they have theatrical auditions coming up. Get a few plays on your resumé. The experience and networking is invaluable.

The Time I Failed At...
My Ill Cat and Other Oscar Bait

The very first representation I signed with was an acting agency in Dayton, Ohio. At this point, I had never auditioned for anything except theatre productions and had never so much as participated in a student film. I got a call from my agent that they were having auditions for an independent film that would be going to the Sundance Film Festival.

I was so excited—my first big break! I got the address from my agent, who told me I could just do a monologue at the audition. I was so excited I didn't even ask about the movie or the role I was auditioning for; my agent probably should have told me, but I also didn't ask. I just found out the timeframe they were seeing people, showed up early, and signed in. When they called my name, I walked into the room and straight to the man sitting at the table, where I handed him my headshot that was not stapled to my resumé.

"Please stand on the mark and go whenever you're ready," the guy said as he looked around the table for a stapler.

"So, my cat has diabetes and it's really sad..." Thus began my witty/tragic monologue about a woman who is waiting for her cat to die whilst testing his pee every day. Gross. Funny. Humiliating. After I finished, the director and the guy manning the camera exchanged glances and said that I could go. I left feeling confident. Happy. Proud of myself for auditioning for a film!

It was only after I had auditioned in LA for a few film projects that I realized my tragic mistake. These people obviously had a script, right? They wouldn't be holding auditions to cast roles if they didn't have characters they were looking for. Why, for heaven's sake, did I not ask what the plot was? I didn't ask for any details whatsoever. For all I know, there could've been dialogue to memorize! What if the film was about heroin junkies? I waltzed in there with my turtleneck sweater and gave a monologue about a cat peeing? Seriously?

Why, Hello, Mrs. Camden

A few years into living in LA, I got a call from my commercial agent about an audition for the heart medication called Plavix. The audition was the same day, so I didn't have too much time to look over the lines they had sent. Usually, you aren't provided with any dialogue for a commercial audition, but this particular spot featured some medical jargon that was particularly tricky to wrap your mouth around. Words like "platelets" and "blood clots" and "cardiovascular." Okay, maybe they weren't that hard in hindsight, but I was memorizing on the fly! The commercial was a young daughter asking her mom to ask the doctor about Plavix.

I arrived at the audition and did my best to memorize the jargon but knew it wasn't word-perfect. The assistant in the lobby told us we could type the dialogue out on our phone if we wanted, since in the actual scenario we are Googling info about Plavix and reading the stats to our mom at a coffee shop. I typed in the text into my phone but didn't realize technology had gotten the best of me and the text didn't save for-some unknown, myserious, infuriating reason.

The time came to be paired up: mother and daughter. The casting director looked at all of us who were in the lobby and began matching blondes with blondes, redheads with redheads. She stood me next to a blonde mom and I turned to greet my new partner and—I almost fell over. It was Catherine Hicks, the mom from the CW's hit show *7th Heaven*. I immediately lost my ability to speak! I tried to remember my lines, but failed miserably. She was so nice, so smiley, so kind. And, hey, she didn't need Plavix! You're Mrs. Camden! Your heart is just fine! I couldn't concentrate. All I kept thinking about was how I used to watch her when I was a little girl and how I didn't want to mess up in front of her.

When it was our turn to go into the room to film, I realized my phone hadn't saved the text. Fortunately, they did have the lines of the script written on a big poster on the side of the wall. *Un*fortunately, I had to stare at that wall the entire time. Fail.

Prepare for anyone to show up and be your scene partner. Figure out a way to put text in your phone where you can count on it being there in case you're encouraged to use such a feature at an audition. Remember that famous actors you admire are just people. After all, Mrs. Camden was auditioning for the part just like I was. And neither of us got it.

People You Should Know

Act Now is a fantastic place to get to know casting directors by taking their workshops. Especially if you don't have representation yet, this is a great way to meet casting directors and pass along your information so they can contact you directly.
Website: www.actnownetwork.com

Alyson Horn is a great person to take workshops from if you want to perfect your commercial audition skills! Her classes hone in on the audition process.
Website: ahccasting.com

Judy Kain teaches a world famous course called "A-Z Commercial Technique." Her classes focus on ALL aspects of commercials, including material for advanced actors and callback work!
Website: Keepitrealacting.com

Here is a website with **contracts** you can duplicate, tweak, and have producers sign to guarantee you will get a copy of booked indie or student films. You'll have to provide your name and email address for the link to download, but the pdf is spot on and will save you a lot of time!
Website: Copyprovided.com

Chapter Seven
Voiceover Work

The voiceover world is the most accessible to actors who do not live in LA. Yes, LA is the voiceover capital of the world, but you can easily receive auditions and submit yourself for projects from anywhere via a wonderful thing called technology. Ten years ago, you could not guarantee yourself even one voiceover audition a year if you lived outside the city, but now, thanks to new web services and home studios, you can do ten auditions a day from Toledo! I'm a new-as-they-come newbie to the voiceover world, but I have wanted to get into it for as long as I've sounded like a cartoon character (which has been my whole life). I've taken several voiceover classes and recently booked a few gigs, and I would love to share what I've learned (and am learning) with you.

Types of Voiceover Work

Any job where you provide voice for a radio, TV, or web spot promoting an idea, company, or product is called commercial work. This is one of the most common jobs available with an endless array of scenarios and characters to portray.

Interactive Voice Response (IVR) is any job where you create phone prompts to help companies divert the flow of incoming calls. You'll make the most money at this type of work (something like $50 per prompt)! Next time you're going batty on your cable company's phone tree, just remember that the voice telling you that you're 1,831st in line made a lot of money doing that! If you'd like to earn thousands of dollars with IVR work, press "3".

Narration work would be on something like a documentary. Calling all Morgan Freemans!

Audiobook work is just what it sounds like: it's getting paid to record books or other publications into mp3 formats for CDs, iPods, equipment for the hearing disabled, and those things they call "cassette tapes." (Ask your parents.)

There are also gigs to be found in specialty narration (medical, technical, scientific, legal), animation and videogame characters, promos ("Huge sale down at Cars Plus!"), and voice-matching. Vocal-matching is essentially being a vocal double. So, if you sound exactly like Jeff Bridges, you're in luck.

Making a Demo

In order to book a voiceover job, you most likely have to have a voiceover demo. A demo is to voiceover work like a headshot and resumé is to acting work. It's your calling card and the only way clients can trust you to do stellar work for their company if you are not already a big celebrity.

All voiceover demos should be no longer than a minute. You could feasibly have a voiceover demo for each of the types of work previously listed, but a commercial demo reel is the most universally accepted demo in place of a type-specific reel. In other words, if you are sending in a submission for a cartoon audition and you don't have an animation demo, they would accept your commercial demo instead. This does not work the other way around; for example, do not turn in an IVR demo when submitting for commercial work.

Most audio companies that produce voiceover demos for actors charge around $1,500, but there are some companies (like the one I use called VO2gogo) that will make a perfectly fine demo for around $700. You can make it yourself, but it's not recommended to do so unless you've been in the voiceover biz for years and can call yourself an expert.

The Services

Once you have your demo made, you can join a voiceover web service called voice123.com to get started with your career. Voice123 is to voiceover work what actorsaccess.com is to acting work. You'll become a member, create a profile describing your voice and the work you'd like to do, and include your demo. You'll immediately begin receiving emails to audition for projects that match your voice type—it's that easy! The cool thing about this site is that you do not need representation. In fact, most companies that are seeking voice talent that use the service have completely cut out the middle man and choose not to use a casting director or agents/managers. They post the job, you submit your reading of their script, and they choose who to book. If you get the job, you record it and email it to them, and they send you a check or pay you via Paypal.

The Technology

It's much easier (and cheaper) than you think to create your own voiceover recording area. It can either be an office in your home or, even better, a walk-in closet. Your walk-in closet will give you the space you need to set up a TV tray big enough for your laptop and mic, but also absorb the excess apartment noises that can clog up your audio tracks in a regular room.

The best type of microphone I recommend to use for a home studio is the Audio-Technica AT2020 USB microphone. This will plug directly into your computer's USB port and it is only about $90 on Amazon.com. Voiceover geniuses have gotten together and discussed the clarity, cost, and quality of this product and agree that you'll be hard-pressed to find a mic that will sound as great or be as easy to use. One voiceover professional I know puts a crew-cut sock from Target over his mic to catch any popping sounds. This guy knows his stuff. I highly recommend you follow suit.

You're going to need a piece of software to edit each clip that you'll be mailing casting directors or clients. A great software program to use is called Audacity, which is easy to navigate and it is free (you could also use Avid Pro Tools or Adobe Audition, but those programs are both complicated and expensive). Audacity works with any microphone that you can plug into your computer via USB and it's compatible with both Mac and PC. You can download the program at audacity.sourceforge.net. Another great option is GarageBand, which comes free on any Mac or can be downloaded as an app for a PC user.

People You Should Know

You can buy sleeves to hand out hard copies of your voiceover demo at a place like Staples or Best Buy, or you could order online in bulk here:

- o *www.uline.com*
- o *www.sleevetown.com*

David Lawrence is brilliant and I highly recommend his voiceover classes. He also makes voiceover demos for actors:

- o *www.vo2gogo.com*
- o *www.vo2gogo.com/classes*

The best microphone to use for voiceover work is the Audio Technica AT2020-usb. If you type that name into amazon.com you'll see the cheapest options, both used and new.

An easy (and free!) program to use to edit together audio clips for a voiceover audition or to put together voiceover demo is called Audacity. You can download it here:
Website: www.Audacity.sourceforge.net
(You can also use a program like GarageBand that comes standard with most Apple products)

Chapter Eight
Marketing

When I moved to LA, I knew next to nothing about what the word "marketing" meant. For some reason, I had it in my mind that a person who works in marketing has to like spreadsheets and matching socks and never goes out on the weekends. Or maybe I had that confused with accounting.

After a stint as an intern in an agent's office, I started to notice the different kinds of mail the agent would receive on a daily basis. It became my job to sort through the various envelopes and packages and pass on what I found to be the most relevant or what I thought the agent may want to see. I realized it would be to my advantage to take note of what made it past my eyes and why. What was the difference between the five mailers I put on her desk and the 75 that I put in the trash? If my own mailings were going to be screened by nobody interns like myself, I wanted to be sure they'd make it past the trash can and onto an agent's desk.

The following marketing tips are a compilation of my own notes from being a mail screener, along with ideas from several marketing workshops I took from casting directors. Enjoy. Long live mismatched socks.

The Purpose of Marketing...

There are plenty of actors who made it in this business who never had to lift a finger to market themselves. There are plenty of actors who market themselves like crazy and still never make it. Now that the disclaimers are out of the way, let it be known that getting your face out there—and doing all the hardcore marketing that you have the time and money for—can really help you get to where you want to be.

...to agents/managers

The purpose of marketing yourself towards agents and managers is exclusively to find representation. No agent means no great auditions. Marketing to them is critical. Many agents and managers are too busy to take phone calls during the day, and offices in LA don't allow you to walk in and advertise yourself in person like they do in New York City. Mail-outs and personal referrals are how a good 90 percent of actors find representation. If you already have an agent and do not wish to find a new one, don't spend your time and money promoting yourself to them.

...to casting directors

The purpose of promoting yourself to casting directors is threefold:

1. To introduce yourself to a casting office who has yet to meet you
2. To remind an office of your existing relationship with them so you stay top-of-mind as a working actor
3. To be polite after an audition by saying "thank you"

Marketing Strategies

After actors meet a casting director for the first time, they are essentially courting that director. You want them to remember you. You want them to think highly of you. Every time I send out a fun announcement (instead of a blank postcard with a boring typed message on the back), I think about what I would do if I were dating this person—or trying to, anyway. I would handwrite that note! I would include some type of gift that was interesting or yummy! I've sent a variety of things in my packages, such as popcorn with a paper popcorn container, chocolate bars with wrappers I made themed to the TV show, lollipops, magnets—you name it. Get creative. It's what will make you memorable.

Imagine what the majority of envelopes look like that cross a casting director's desk every day. Manila. White. Tan. Pizza coupons. White. More manila. If the agent or director only has time to open five things, how can you make sure your piece of mail is one of those five? By being different!

I strongly encourage you to find brightly colored envelopes if you're sending cards. If you're sending out a mailing for agents or managers, it should include a brief cover letter and a head-shot/resumé. You could even mail this kind of package in a clear envelope so they can see your face before the envelope is even opened! The idea here is to be as creative and attractive as possible with your packaging in the hopes yours will be picked up before others.

I had a casting director tell me that she picks up her mail once a week and dumps the huge box out on her office table. She said sometimes she receives over 400 pieces of mail each week! Since she is a busy lady with two small kids at home, what she does to save time is to look at the pile and pick things out that attract her eye. She scouts out the ones that look like they contain something other than just a piece of paper. If the package pops out a little bit, she is curious to know what the mailing contains. Is it candy? Is it a ceramic monkey? Who knows?

Send Eye-Catching Postcards

If you don't have the money to send out clever packaging, don't get too stressed. Many actors have postcards printed with a generic front and blank back. The front of the postcard would contain their name, representation contact info (or, if you don't have any representation, your personal contact info), unions they belong to, and at least two headshots with different looks/types. You could use postcards for:

- A mass mailing, sending one postcard to every casting director or agent you'd like to meet. On the back, personalize it with a handwritten note.
- A "thank you" to the VIP you met at an audition, casting director workshop, or acting class.
- An announcement for a big upcoming job you've booked.

From a marketing standpoint, don't be afraid to get creative in your headshot when you're seeking representation by an agent or manager. I ran across some photos of a young twenty-something girl who was looking for an agent, and I still remember her pictures to this day. She drew a big sign with colorful markers that said "seeking representation" with an arrow pointing towards her face. She had a silly laugh, cute glasses and sweet eyes. If I were an agent and had room on my agency's roster, I definitely would have at least given her an interview.

I do have general postcards printed up so that I can toss one at anyone I might randomly meet that I feel should have my contact info. (Think of these as business cards for actors.) Other than that, I always try to make postcards for specific purposes, like a *Criminal Minds* postcard announcing my episode air date. If I were seeking representation, I would do something cute like the girl who was holding a poster in her photo, saying I was agent shopping. Generic postcards are appreciated and seen by offices, but do what you can to stand out as much as possible.

I suggest doing general postcard mailings once every 3-6 months. Make sure you print them with your photograph and your name, along with a few newsworthy bullet points like, "My website is up-and-running!" or "Catch me in Playhouse West's upcoming theater season as Eugene in *Broadway Bound*" or "I just had a baby!" or "I went from brunette to bald!"

Write and Send Great Cover Letters

When you're sending out a headshot/resumé for agents or casting directors to get to know you, it's important to include a cover letter that helps them form an opinion about you. You want to keep it short and to the point! Industry professionals are busy people, so the shorter you can keep your letter the more likely they are to skim it or even read it completely.

Don't include a cover letter with a postcard blast. But I do recommend including a cover letter if you're mailing paper sized envelopes to submit yourself for a role unsolicited, introduce yourself to a casting director, or request a meeting with an agent. It's professional and helpful!

Leave enough space after your typed name to sign the cover letter with a pen once you've printed it. I think this gives a personal touch and shows them that you're specifically reaching out to them.

Find out if the recipient is male or female and triple-check the spelling of every name. You can imagine why this is important. Be sure you know exactly what your recipient does. Are they an agent? Remember, agents don't cast you, so it would be a mistake to use language like, "I hope you can find me a part..." Are they a casting director? They don't have clients, so it would be silly to say, "I'd love to be represented by you." Prove to them how smart you are by showing that you know who they are and what they do by doing your homework before you write the letter.

Any big pieces of information you'd like to share (like a role you just booked, or maybe you just had a baby, or just moved here from a foreign country) should be brief and start right away within the first two sentences. This introduces you to them and shows them why they should pay attention to you.

If someone referred you to this individual, mention that right away in the body of text or even in the subject line! (Make sure that they've actually referred you, don't just drop a name because you feel like it.)

You must include multiple ways for them to contact you. (What if you eventually change cell phone numbers? An email address is canceled? Don't miss a chance to connect with them.) Also, try to show your personality even though your letter is professional and brief.

I've included several sample cover letters at the end of this chapter to give you an idea of what they can look like. There are many opinions on cover letters, many templates, and many ways to format them.

Create a Database

Create a database where you can store all the information for your auditions. For every casting director that calls you in, make sure you record their name and address and the date you saw them. I have a spiral-bound book where I record each appointment, and then I transfer that information to a spreadsheet. (If you're like me, it's possible you'll lose this notebook once or twice, so always have a second hard copy or electronic copy somewhere.)

Make (and Keep) Connections

Find local organizations you can plug into and start attending their weekly or monthly meetings. It's vital for actors to network with one another; you never know who you're going to meet. Also, actors who have been in town longer than you can give you valuable advice: which classes are a waste of time, which coffee houses certain casting directors frequent, which hair salons give discounts to SAG members, etc.

It's likely that the state or city you're moving from has a group already formed and waiting for you! I've plugged into the Nebraska Coast Connection and have learned so much about the industry—and made some great new Husker friends to boot!

Once you meet someone in the industry, ask him or her for a business card or contact info. Add their names to your database immediately when you get home and be sure to keep your entries updated so your list is current when it comes time to send out that big announcement.

Say "Thank You"

Always be sure to say thank you to casting directors who call you in or help you book a job. A simple note that says "thank you" will go a long way toward making you memorable. Keeping yourself at the front of everyone's mind is what you're going for, and the more excuses you have to send something their way (with your picture on it, of course) the better. I always make the "thanks" a little bigger when it's a booking rather than just an audition, like sending chocolates or fruit or something special.

Act at Events for Free

If you can, offer to act at events for free! If you know people doing a fundraiser or a showcase, give them a call to see if they need a monologue or a standup routine. Maybe someone is planning to do a video promo for the event at a local college campus or church. Maybe an organization close by needs a host for an awards night or an auction. Not only do these types of things allow you to practice your acting for stage and film, they help get your name out there. The more people see you, the better the chance that someone in the audience can book you for a job.

Start a Blog

Start your own blog. Believe it or not, the life of an actor, struggling or successful, makes for quite an interesting read. The more people you have following your story, the more likely it is that someone in a position to recommend you for a booking will stumble upon your site. There are currently over 150 million bloggers on the Internet. Never, ever, ever say anything bad about something or someone, like a bad audition site, mean directors, high-maintenance actors, etc. That stuff doesn't ever leave the Internet, and a simple "Google Alert" will let casting directors know the second someone uses their name on the Internet. Not worth it, friend. Vent to your mom. Or your cat.

Social Networking

If you've been boycotting social media outlets, it's time to face the music and stop being such a pansy. You'll seriously miss out on a wealth of opportunity to advertise yourself if you're not willing to create accounts with places like Facebook, LinkedIn, and Twitter. I thought Myspace was passé and only joined when I did the premiere of the play *Spring Awakening* in LA. A cast member created an account for the production and each actor was featured along with our headshots and resumés. The promotion strategy worked and fans that frequented our page showed up at the show to purchase tickets. Not only that, assistant directors I had worked with doing background for television found my account and messaged me with offers for more work. Awesome! Now I've long since given up my Myspace account (so long, 2007), but I think you can get my point here. If casting directors and other industry people use a form of social media, then you should, too!

A year after Spring Awakening, shortly after one of my *Starstruck* mailings, I got a message through my Facebook fan page from a casting agency.

> "Hi, I am working the casting office for [a major TV show] and just got your shiny purple self-submission. I was sure that whoever sent it was too cute to set aside. I was right. Also, I am impressed by how you strive to get your face out there on your own, even though you have proper representation. Thank you very much for the Valentine's Day candy and Starbursts (my favorite)! Unfortunately, you're a bit too young for [our current opportunities]. But when something comes up, I will be sure to get you in to meet with the head casting director in the future. Congrats to you on *Starstruck*."

See? This worked, too. They had never met me, but they liked my packaging, opened it, found my personality charming, and enjoyed it (or maybe the Starbursts) so much that they took the time to find me on Facebook and contact me. Neat, huh?

Make a Website

The decision to create an acting website for myself was a big one. I had seen other actors' websites but had never pursued a site of my own until I ran across a photography site I fell in love with. The company (bludomain.com) specializes in making websites for photographers, but something clicked in my brain and I knew the templates they provided would look amazing for actors as well. I'm so glad I made the decision to create one!

Fortunately, there are a lot of companies that will provide templates for you, and all you have to do is fill in the blanks! I am not very computer or design savvy, but they make it easy. It's really a matter of typing in the titles of the pages that you have and uploading images, just like you're attaching something to an email. I've recommended a few of these sites at the end of this chapter.

When you do decide to create a website, the main headings on your home page should be photos (headshots), resumé, and contact info. If you'd like to add a bio section with your story and a glimpse of your personality, that's great! Include a reel if you have one. One idea is to have a section called "Reviews" where you can put blurbs from newspaper critics who (positively!) mention your performance by name. (Don't forget to cite those sources.) Be as creative as you want, but you must include the major categories I've listed or your homepage won't be as effective as you hoped.

If you have a family member or friend who can design a website, that's great, but use caution. A close friend of mine was given an acting website for his birthday from his web-developer brother, who promised to be the administrator. It became complicated after a year or two when my friend would want to update the resumé or photos on the site and his brother couldn't even remember the administrator password. Of course, your family and friends will have good intentions, but what happens if you get a new set of photos you'd like to update for a big audition next week, and they're busy for a month straight? It is for these reasons that I think it's best if you own and control all aspects of your site so that you can add to or change your pages at any time.

Having a website is a super convenient way to submit yourself for non-union projects online. Before I became SAG, I would constantly submit myself for side-projects using my website. When the audition notice provided an email address for me to send an attached headshot and resumé, I simply emailed back with my name, what character I was interested in, and "Here is a link to my website where you'll find my headshots, updated resumé, and other fun stuff." I was able to send twice the number of submissions by copy/pasting that line and link into the body of an email instead of taking the time to mail material hardcopy or attaching them one-by-one for each submission.

If you do decide to create a website, having a logo will help you to appear more established and professional. I include my logo as a sticker on everything that I mail out. Consider what colors and design styles match both your personality and the kind of characters you play well.

Sample Cover Letter for an Agent #1

September 4, 2017

Nora Wenzel
10298 Fantastic Place
Anywhere City, CA
234-345-6678
Thisisfake@email.com

ABC Agency
4444 Four Drive
Beverly Hills, CA 90210

To: Mr. Matthew Corliss
Re: Seeking Representation

Dear Mr. Corliss,

I'm new to Los Angeles and wanted to let you know that I just booked a supporting role in the Santa Monica Playhouse's production of Annie. I am currently taking meetings with theatrical agents and wanted to be sure to introduce myself to you because I've heard great things about your agency. You'll find my headshot and resumé enclosed. Looking forward to hearing from you!

Cheers,

Nora Wenzel

Nora Wenzel

Sample Cover Letter for an Agent #2

September 4, 2017

Nora Wenzel
10298 Fantastic Place
Anywhere City, CA
234-345-6678
Thisisfake@email.com

The Brooks Agency
Who Dat Drive
Hollywood, CA 91604

Attn: Ms. Rebecca Brooks
Re: Referred by Stacy McFall

Dear Ms. Brooks,

I met Stacy McFall during a callback for Mickey's Big Adventure, and she suggested that I reach out to you. I just moved to town from Springfield, MO and am currently shopping for both a commercial and theatrical agent. Stacy says you're fantastic at both! You'll find my resumé and headshot included for your review.

Sincerely,

Nora Wenzel

Nora Wenzel

Sample Cover Letter for a Casting DIrector

September 4, 2017

Nora Wenzel
10298 Fantastic Place
Anywhere City, CA
234-345-6678
Thisisfake@email.com

To: Mr. Corey Ellis
Re: Submission for the role of 'Ella' in *CSI*

Dear Mr. Ellis,

You mentioned in the breakdown for 'Ella' in CSI that scuba-diving experience is a must. Just writing to let you know that I am a certified diver and have worked for both Sea World and California Parks and Rec for five years. I also just finished Scott Miller's *Meisner Technique* acting class in Santa Monica!

I've enclosed a resumé and headshot for your consideration.

Looking forward to hearing from you,

Nora Wenzel

Nora Wenzel

What You Can Do Right Now

o Being Photoshop savvy will help you in designing your postcards. Take some basic courses, watch any of the countless video tutorials online, or ask to trade a photographer friend some gift certificates to watch and learn from them. Some basic knowledge can go a long way.

o Start compiling a list of people you have previously met and would like to contact when you send out your first mailing.

o Browse the Internet for possible website designers or websites where you can design and manage your own site or purchase design templates. Companies I know and like include: Bludomain, WIX, and WordPress.

o Start brainstorming possible logo ideas and begin to brand yourself. Remember, a logo may be the first impression people get of you when they visit your website or open a piece of mail.

People You Should Know

Visit **Samuel French** stores (*SamuelFrench.com*) for great options on finding contact information for agents and casting director mailings. Two books/pamphlets Samuel French carries with addresses for a mailing:

- *The Right Agent* (updated every month, $10.00)
- *Casting Director Guide* (updated every two months, $13.00)

OR subscribe to **Castingabout.com** to sort and print your own labels via the internet. (This, however, would be to market to casting offices only, not representation)

Another online option for finding agent/manager addresses: ***www.sag.org/content/find-agent***

Shiny (purple, green, pink, you name it!) mailing packages: ***www.uline.com***

Postcards (Flat greeting cards at this site are cheaper than postcards, and they're the same thing): ***uprinting.com/flat-greeting-cards.html***

Headshot printing: ***reproductions.com***

Envelopes for mailing headshots:

- ***www.envelopemall.com***
- ***www.uline.com***

Chapter Nine
Getting Paid

As I mentioned at the very beginning of this book, you better not set out to pursue this biz because you want to get rich. Seriously. I want to be as honest with you as possible about the money side of this, because there's a good chance you might misunderstand the reality of it just like I did. Hollywood has a way of glamorizing itself, and it's easy to watch and assume that we will all be rich and famous after we work on a TV show or two. Not true. Not even close.

The reality is this: it's possible that you would make more money in a workweek from babysitting or Starbucks than working once as a co-star on a television episode. After taxes and commissions, it's possible to bring home as little as $400 for a day of *principal* work, and that, my friends, will not pay the rent. Or feed the cat.

That's the financial negative end of the spectrum, and, of course, you've seen the positive end everywhere from entertainment biographies to tabloid covers. Is it possible to make millions the longer you do this? Absolutely. Does it happen for everyone? No. Does it happen for even half? No. Even a quarter? NO.

In this chapter, I'll break down the current minimum payments for paid (union) theatre, television, and film work according to union contracts. As you're processing this, realize that, depending on your resumé and representation's negotiating skills, your rate could be higher.

Theatre

For Equity theatre, you can earn anywhere from $200-$1,000 per week, or more depending on which contract the theater has signed with AEA and how many shows you are contracted to perform in. The weekly pay can be much higher, but that depends on your agent's negotiating skills, your individual talent, and the notoriety of the production or role. Non-Equity theatre is usually unpaid, but you'll occasionally come across a theater willing to pay a small stipend ($20-$100) to actors for each rehearsal and/or show. Los Angeles theatres often use an Equity 99-seat Plan, where small theatres under 99 seats hire union or non-union actors, and pay them nine dollars per show. Don't spend it all in one place!

Film/TV

For TV SAG/AFTRA projects, you'll get paid for filming the show, as well as an equal amount for the first time the project reruns. The second time the show reruns, you'll get paid again, but a little less. Any re-airings after that will pay significantly less each time. For film, an actor's pay rate depends on the contract with the producers, the size of your role, etc. But as long as the film is making money for the producers, you will see a paycheck! You won't make any residuals for extra/background work.

Here are the current minimum SAG rates for Union actors:

- o Day rate for day player: $809
- o Day rate for background actor: $139
- o Day rate for photo-double: $149
- o Day rate for stand-in: $154
- o Choreographed swimmers/skaters: $322
- o Weekly rate (five days): $2,808
- o Weekly rate (five days) for series regular: $3,377

Weekly rates are a bargain that the unions have worked out for the producers so production doesn't have to pay actors five times the daily rate ($809) for five consecutive days of employment. Remember that just because you're on hold and paid for a full five days of filming doesn't mean they will use you every day, it's possible that they could use you for two or three days and still pay you for the week, depending on the project. You'll learn more about how much it will cost to join the union and see website links to current contracts and rates in chapter ten.

Overtime

For union and non-union, the regular workday is eight consecutive hours, excluding meal breaks. Every hour you work over that is considered overtime and you get a higher rate of pay. Hours 9-12 are called "time and a half," and you get 1.5 times your hourly rate. Each hour of work after the 12th hour is called "double time," and you multiply your hourly rate by two. This adds up faster than you can imagine! There is also a rare and magical pay rate called "golden time": every hour after the 16th, you get your entire day rate of pay each and every hour. I've only reached this a few times (including once on a TV show when a famous actress was 17 hours late!). The "golden time" is rare and it feels like you're committing highway robbery. Glorious.

Paying Your Representation

If you're union, your agent's commission will be no more than 10 percent. Managers usually ask for 10 or 15 percent. If you're non-union, you have no one to protect you against representation asking for a higher percentage. Make sure you read your contract very carefully and understand the commission rate.

Commission rates are taken off the gross amount of your total check. In other words, if you were paid $100 and taxes took out $30 (thank you, California), your representation's commission would be based on the initial $100 pay—not the $70 you went home with. They would each get $10.

Most agencies will require you to sign a waiver when you agree to be their client, which means they will receive all your paychecks directly. The agency will then send your manager (if you have one) a check for what you owe them, plus a check to you with the remaining balance (after they take out your taxes and commissions). Some agencies do not ask you to sign a waiver, and you are responsible to write personal checks and send along a photocopied paystub for their accounting purposes. Each agency and management company is different, though, and understandably, most will require all checks to go through them to ensure that they are properly paid for their work.

Chapter Ten

Unions 101

If you're not familiar with the way unions work, you may be asking yourself, "What's the point?" A union ensures that the person who hires you has to pay you what you were promised to be paid and not a penny less. Unions negotiate minimum pay for an actor, which allows people like you and I to make a living doing this crazy thing. They make deals on behalf of their members for important things like health insurance, pension plans, and retirement. If there are consistent problems amongst their members, they'll take new issues to the bargaining table and iron out solutions with producers when they next negotiate.

For example, thanks to unions, every six hours you're required to be given a meal or, at the very least, the opportunity to eat. If a director is pushing to finish a shot, you get paid a "meal penalty" for every 15 minutes you aren't excused from set to eat. Thank SAG that happens, or you'd be working thirteen hours straight without food!

In short, a union protects you, and you'll find it quite impossible to imagine living without them once you've joined up. Union is the way to go.

There are two unions that actors can join:
1. SAG/AFTRA (Screen Actors Guild/American Federation of Television and Radio Artists)
2. AEA (Actors Equity Association, often just referred to as "Equity")

If you want to act in professional theatre for a living, New York City is definitely the town to pursue. There most certainly are union theatre productions in LA, but nowhere near the caliber and quantity of productions in New York. Most industry professionals (including actors!) will admit that if you really want to make a living at acting, film and TV are the true moneymakers.

SAG/AFTRA is the giant union in Hollywood that represents actors. It's difficult to get into and definitely well respected. Nine times out of ten, you won't be able to get a big audition for a TV show or film unless you are union and have a great agent. Some great agents do represent non-union actors, but most of the time you can't get fantastic representation until you are in SAG. That's why getting into SAG is the hottest ticket in town!

Because I've chosen to spend most of my time pursing film and TV (instead of theatre), I'll spend the next few pages focusing on the details of SAG/AFTRA.

Getting into SAG

"How did you get into SAG?" That is the question I asked the most before I was in the union, and it's the one I hear most often now that I've joined. Everyone has a different story, and, as an actor on the outside looking in, it's a deep question that constantly eats at you. It can be incredibly frustrating when you know that some actors were able to join SAG within two weeks of moving to LA, while others have been here for five years and are still trying to join. All I can advise is to have patience. Know that all the frustration is worth it when you hold that union card in your hands for the first time!

There are three primary ways to become eligible to join SAG.

#1: Perform in a Principal Role in TV or Film

The first way to earn your way into SAG is to land a principal role in TV or film. One role and—poof!—you're in. The trick is landing a principal role as a non-union actor.

If you have a spoken line in a TV show or a SAG film, that means you have a principal role. As a non-union actor, it's frustrating to realize, "Okay, I can't get a principal role unless I go to major auditions... and I can't get major auditions until I'm in SAG...and I can't get into SAG unless I have a principal role..." So frustrating, right? Be encouraged because there are ways to conquer this catch-22.

Occasionally, casting directors will be looking for something unique and will open their auditions up to the non-union crowd. If, for example, casting needs to find a young Angelina Jolie or a young Bryan Cranston, they'd realize their chances of coming across a look-alike child are greater the more children they're able to audition. Perhaps they're looking for a circus performer who is also fluent in a difficult language. Anything that may be harder to find has a better chance of getting a non-union breakdown for auditions.

Perhaps the creator of a show or the director for a film really wants to find an "unknown" to fill a role. Sometimes shows will hold national auditions in different cities to create "buzz" about a certain project. They may not happen all the time, but you'll see notices on the Internet for those more than you might expect if you're looking for them.

I've also seen background actors bumped up to principal status while on the set. Perhaps a director has realized that there really should be a line explaining why the main character is running late or the bellman should say "thank you" or the cop should yell, "Hold it right there!" For any number of reasons, if you happen to be standing in the right place at the right time, an expected paycheck of $60 could turn into $960 in a matter of seconds. On top of that, you'd be given a principal contract to sign on your way out of the studio lot, and you'd be eligible to join SAG.

#2: Work Three Days as a SAG Extra

The second way to become SAG-eligible is to earn three SAG vouchers by working three days as a SAG extra. This takes a lot of patience and a little luck, but is probably the most common way for actors to earn their way into SAG.

Background actors are called "extras" and they are the people hired to fill the scenes behind the principal performers. If you've ever seen a scene at a restaurant where two people are discussing something over dinner, you've definitely seen at least thirty extras without realizing it. The waitress walking by. The host seating people on the left. The mother taking her baby to the bathroom. The bartender polishing a glass. This is the reality created to make the scene believable, and it takes a village—of extras—to make it happen.

The first year I was in LA, I did nothing but community theatre by night and extra work by day. I wanted to learn as much as I possibly could by being on set. Who is the "2nd 2nd" and what is their job? What does "check the gate" and "back to one" mean? All these things (and about a billion more) I learned from being an extra.

Check out the glossary at the back of the book to learn some terms that I think will be helpful!

When you work as an extra, right when you arrive on set and check in with the designated production staff (usually this is the 2nd 2nd AD), they'll give you a voucher. A voucher is your contract for the day and has a place to fill out all your personal information. It will contain the name of the production, your name, and the role you're playing (football player, lawyer, pedestrian, nurse, etc). You fill in where you want your check to be sent and the hours that you worked. At the end of the day, you will sign out with the same staff member and keep a copy of the voucher.

If you are non-union, your voucher will be blue. All SAG vouchers are yellow. If you're really serious about becoming a professional actor, your goal is to get three yellow vouchers.

Every show on TV (not including realtiy television) has to have a contract with the actor's union, SAG/AFTRA. Union contracts stipulate that a certain percentage of all actors on set must be SAG members; the exact number is determined based on the film's size (i.e. budget, cast, etc.) If a SAG extra doesn't show up to work that day—or a few other hundred serendipitous scenarios occur—you might become eligible for a union voucher.

Here are a few examples of how that can happen:

Scenario One: A SAG extra that was originally booked had to cancel at the last minute or is late to set. According to the production contract, they must employ a specific number of SAG actors, so the production staff member will choose someone to upgrade to union status. They will take your blue voucher away and give you the yellow one instead. You will then cross out the missing actor's name and replace it with your own. Once you do this three separate times, you're eligible to join SAG!

Scenario Two: You are called back to set for the next day of shooting because of where you were standing in a shot they have to match. Perhaps you were seated in the bleachers at a football game right behind the principal actors, and they had one day to do all the wide crowd shots. Shoots often go longer than expected and scenes or shots have to be pushed to the next day. If they're filming "close-ups" on the principal actors the second day, they would need to match who was in the frame the day before. If that day of shooting requires a smaller amount of background actors (and one of them has to be you!), chances are a yellow voucher will be yours.

Scenario Three: You work one day as a stand-in. A stand-in is an extra who usually matches a principal actor in height and hair color. The stand-in will literally stand on the actor's mark. Depending on the director's style, the stand-in may or may not be asked to say the actor's dialogue, though they will usually do the blocking that the actor will perform in the scene. This helps the lighting and camera crews to do all their major setup without the actor having to be present. This way, the actor can get their hair and makeup finished, take notes from the director, memorize their lines and not "hold their chin up a little higher so the grip can determine where his bounce casts a shadow." That's the stand-in's job! You can book a job as a stand-in by being pulled from the non-union crowd once you arrive on set, or you can book the job the day before with your background company via your photos and height info. Stand-ins always get paid a little more and usually work on a yellow SAG voucher.

I earned my three SAG vouchers on the show *Gilmore Girls.* I had been regularly working as a non-union extra for the show as a townsperson of the show's fictitious town, Stars Hollow. I got to know the 2nd AD really well because every time the script required an outside shot in the town, I was there! I did my best to always have a stellar attitude, always listen to directions, never

149

talk while filming, and follow the simple rules (like no cell phones on set). After a long day of filming, she came up to me and told me they had to push a scene to the following workday because they'd run out of daylight. She asked me if I was interested in working the next day, but I already had plans, so I told her I was unavailable. She smiled at me and said, "Would you be willing to change your plans if I gave you a SAG voucher?" I'd been working for four solid months as an extra and had never even come close to being offered one. "Are you kidding? Tell me my call time and I'm there!"

My second voucher came shortly after the first. I was again working as a non-union townsperson on the show, and the 2nd AD approached me early that morning and pulled me aside.

"How tall are you?"

"Five-two."

"Have you ever worked as a stand-in before?"

"Um...no."
"Would you like to?"

Before or after I pee my pants with excitement?

"Of course!"

Turns out, the stand-in that was supposed to be on set for Sally Struthers had called in sick, and I was only one of three blondes working that day. And, what do you know, Sally and I are even the same height!

Two down, one to go. I went for about a month without work on *Gilmore Girls* because there were no outside Stars Hollow shots planned in those episodes. I heard there was going to be a large call for extras for a graduation scene, so I decided to try and spec a day of background work.

When you spec for a show, you show up at the same time and place where other background actors are being called, and you wait to see if someone doesn't show up. Most often the PA or 2nd 2nd checking in the extras will start a spec sign-in sheet and they will take people as they have room in the order that people have signed up. Almost all large calls (50+ extras) are guaranteed to have someone running late, and you're a shoe-in for calls that require 100 or more. I crossed my fingers and hoped that some silly SAG extra would not feel like attending the main character Rory's graduation. My new friend, the 2nd AD, saw me sitting on the ground near the line of extras waiting to check in.

"Are you going to be a graduate today, Abbie?"

"Oh, I'm just spec-ing. I'm trying to get that third voucher!"

"You haven't gotten your third one yet? Well, we love you. We'll help you out if you don't get one today."

My heart leapt and I grinned like an idiot. Turns out, that day there were people who didn't show up for work, but they happened to be working on a non-union voucher. I was able to take their place and was still upbeat thinking about the conversation that happened that morning. The following week I received a phone call from the extras casting company I worked with.

"Hey Abbie, *Gilmore Girls* production called, and they'd like you to stand-in for [the character of] Paris tomorrow, can you make it? It's their last day of filming on the last season." And that, my friends, is how I got my third voucher.

My advice to you? Be as polite and positive as possible on set. Know the names of the PA's who are in charge of you and respect them. Be available and willing. Don't complain. Follow the rules. These things sound ridiculously stupid for me to say, but you'd be surprised how many background actors do the opposite. And you'd be pleasantly surprised to find how much you'll stand out as a professional if you make these suggestions part of your everyday routine.

#3: Be in an Affiliated Union and Land a Principal Role

The third and final way to become eligible for SAG is to be a member of an affiliated union, such as ACTRA, AEA, AGMA, or AGVA for one year, and then work as a principal actor for one day. If you do that, you become eligible to join SAG. If you're stuck in a rut and itching for a way to join SAG because scenarios one and two haven't panned out for you, paying to join one of these sister unions first and then joining SAG after that year could be the way to go. It sounds easy, but remember, you must book a role as a principle performer (have lines!) for one of those unions during that year to qualify.

Being SAG-Eligible

Just because you are eligible to join SAG does not mean that you must join. Your resumé can say "SAG-E" or "SAG ELIGIBLE" at the top and people will understand that that means you have earned your way into the union but you have not paid to join yet. At any time you could walk in to the SAG building, pay your initiation fee and dues, and be a member but, for some reason, you are choosing not to.

Some people choose not to because they don't have the money. SAG currently costs a one-time initiation fee of $3,000, which requires some prior financial planning (or a rich and generous uncle). There are also annual fees of about $188 you'll have to pay up front, so you'll need about $3,200 altogether when you decide it's time to get that SAG card. (Remember that after booking a job you'll owe SAG about 2 percent of your paychecks.)

Some people decide not to join right away because they want to build up their resumé first with non-union projects before diving into SAG work as a small fish in a huge pond of actors with legitimate union credits. If you don't have any film or TV credits, it's a good idea to wait to join SAG. Get some of those student and indie films on there, get a reel started, and then join up!

People You Should Know

Central Casting is the biggest EXTRAS company in LA (and the one I used to book background work which got me into SAG):
Website: www.centralcasting.org

To research current union payment rates and agreements, visit:

- *www.actorsequity.org/agreements*
- *www.sagaftra.org/production-center*

Websites for actor unions:

- SAG/AFTRA: www.sagaftra.org
- Equity: www.actorsequity.org

Chapter Eleven
The Spiritual Side of Things

There is a spiritual side to being a creative artist. If you choose to ignore that, you do so at your own risk. I can't imagine what my life as an actor would be like if I did not have my faith. The rejection in this industry, the constant drain on your emotions, and the brutality of being in the trenches in this town will all deflate your dreams in a heartbeat if you don't have something solid to fall back on.

You may not be a religious person. You may not be comfortable with the idea of being "spiritual." You may not even know what you believe. If that's true, I challenge you to figure out what you do believe before you make the move to pursue the industry. Do some homework. Do some soul searching. You really must be grounded in who you are and what you believe if you're going to survive in this industry, never mind be successful in it.

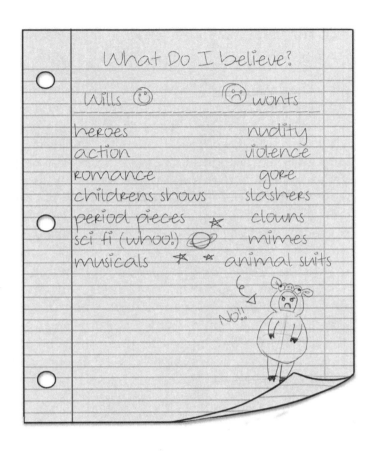

Remaining Grounded: Write it Down

Write it down. Not even joking. Write down a list of things you believe in and why. What are your truths? What are your non-negotiables? Fill a page with sentences that begin with "I believe…"

and don't lose it because you're going to need to come back to it for a reminder again and again.

Write a second list that includes things you're not willing to do for your career. For example, my list includes "no nudity." I absolutely will not do nudity on stage or film—ever. I say write it down before you pursue this business (and keep that list close by) because it's very easy to forget your values when you have a shiny golden opportunity thrown in your face. In that moment, it will be tempting to compromise your values for something that seems like it will make your life so much better. So write it down now, while you're of sober mind, to figure out what compromises simply are not worth that golden opportunity, no matter what it promises to do for you. If you don't have something solid to hold your feet to the floor, you'll be swept away and begin to make a series of poor decisions. Eventually, you'll realize you strayed from the very beliefs that made you who you were when you first dreamed of being an actor. This list will help you identify red flags.

Recognizing red flags is the most important thing you can do to keep Hollywood from changing who you are as a person and help you retain those moral strengths that you possess. You have to know what you will and won't do first. Only then can you face situations you are confronted

159

with that challenge who you are and what you believe.

Note: Be very careful of postings on Craigslist.com or other sites that post "modeling jobs" that seem to suggest there will be little clothing involved. At best, these are adult films looking for inexpensive actors. At worst, these are dangerous people looking to lure vulnerable actors and actresses.

Your List Isn't a Secret

Once you've figured out your non-negotiables, make sure you don't allow those to catch any potential directors off-guard. It's your responsibility to be clear from the very beginning if there is even a chance you could have an issue with content. You can't get into the middle of filming and announce, "Oh, by the way, I can't say these particular words" or "I won't even pretend I'm doing this."

A friend of mine from school had a rule of "no kissing." She was also an actress (and a talented one, at that!) and her stance was that, if a director really wanted her, they would work something out. This isn't true in Hollywood, per se, but this was just a school play. It was *Beauty and the Beast*, and my lovely and talented friend landed the lead romantic role of Belle. However, she failed to mention to the director and casting staff about her "no kissing" rule until rehearsals had been going on for some time. When it came time to rehearse the final scene where, of course, there is that magical climactic kiss that ends the story, the beans were spilled. How in the world can the Beast turn into a prince at the end of the story without a kiss? A magical...hug, maybe? The director kindly let her Belle know that, had they known about her rule, they would have cast someone else; of course, it was too late to do that now. They were stuck in a very uncomfortable situation. Graciously, the director decided to accommodate her rule instead of forcing the actress playing Belle to compromise, and the entire cast and crew's hard work culminated in a final scene with a—wait for it—"thumb kiss." As in, the actor playing Beast slipped his thumb over Belle's lips just before he planted the big one...on himself.

While "no kissing" is not one of my personal rules, I respect my friend for her conviction. If my friend valued her rule over the role, all the more power to her. In fact, that is exactly what I'm advocating for. However, let me be very clear: She should have made that choice clear *before* being cast—and she should have turned down the role. Luckily things worked out for her, but imagine what would've happened if the director hadn't been so willing to compromise? She would've either had to do something she was against or been kicked out of the production. Fat chance of being cast again by the same director that fires you, right?

If you want to set standards that are different from others, that is absolutely okay. But don't audition for a part that requires you to break that rule. If you know that a role requires nudity and you know you will never do nudity, you would be a fool to walk into the audition room and waste everyone's time. When things start to approach the gray areas, be brave and state your personal standards with conviction. Just don't wait until it's too late. Odds are, your director won't be nearly as understanding as dear Belle's if you wait to take a stand three weeks into production.

The Catch-22 of TV Series

One-episode co-star and guest star roles are included in the "read the material before you commit to the project" camp. But when you're a recurring co-star, guest star, or series regular on episodic TV, it gets a bit sticky. These are the exception to the rule—you obviously can't read all the episodes planned for your character if the writers haven't written them yet.

The best suggestion I have if you're in this place is to get an idea from the writers, producers, or director, (or whoever is available to answer questions) what the arc of your character will be. Comb through the scenes you are provided with to get a feel for the character *of* your character— if you will.

For my *90210* recurring guest star role, I had lengthy conversations with the producers about my character, Emily. They explained that she arrived in Beverly Hills as a sweet and charming Kansas gal, but the high-society zip code changed her into something more devious. I was not privy to the details of the ending of my role on the show, but I did know that Emily would be learning some valuable lessons about friendship and honesty before leaving Beverly Hills because of her mistakes. It was clear that her devious ways were going to have some very realistic consequences that she was going to have to deal with. So, although I didn't have access to the script itself, I knew the material would be aligned with decisions I had made about content and character portrayal.

Keep in mind that most episodic TV is daytime or primetime TV, which have strict ratings and content limitations. There will not be an excess of cursing (and certainly none of the PG-13 words you may want to avoid on national TV) and there won't be any nudity, if the show you're auditioning for broadcasts on network TV. The exceptions to standard rules and ratings are HBO, Showtime, Cinemax, or STARZ shows, which require subscriptions and do not censor any adult material.

Black and White and Gray

Young actors and actresses email me all the time about particular projects or roles, wanting a concrete answer about what they should accept or decline. I know this may be disappointing to hear, but there is rarely a black-and-white answer. It's a big, fat, gray area, and many people will have different thoughts and opinions— which is why it's so important for you to create boundaries.

I will tell you how I personally approach projects. I'm not saying it's the right way; it's just how I personally do it. Basically, I sit down and contemplate a role by asking the question, "Does this role glorify evil?" In other words, "Will the audience be rooting for the poor decisions I'm making, or will they see the consequences of wrong choices?" (Obviously, you're really going to have to figure out what "evil" and "wrong" is to you—or else this might get confusing.)

Let's take a look at two plays you may be familiar with: *A Streetcar Named Desire* by Tennessee Williams and the Bob Fosse musical *Chicago*. *Streetcar* features a woman in the leading role named Blanche who is as trashy as they come. She is manipulative and promiscuous, taking advantage of whomever she can with her selfishness. However (spoiler alert!), Blanche goes crazy in the end and is carted off to an insane asylum. She is destroyed by her actions and has hurt most of the people in her life as well. What does the audience take away? That wreckless behavior and poor decisions have negative consequences. So, even though Blanche is a rather horrible person, it would be consistent with my values to accept this role.

In *Chicago,* the two leading ladies are adulteress murderers. Yes, the music is fantastic and the dancing is jaw-dropping and those roles are an actress' dream. But the audience is left rooting for the two women the entire time, hoping they can "razzle dazzle" (or, cheat) the law to literally get away with adultery and murder. For this reason, personally, I would have a hard time reconciling these roles with my values. Even though Roxie from *Chicago* and Blanche from *Streetcar* are basically the same type of character, I would only accept Blanche if I had a chance to do both.

Almost every story needs conflict to teach a lesson, and I get that. Even the Bible. The Bible is absolutely full of stories about people making poor decisions: rape, murder, suicide, rebellion, manipulation, and deceit, just to name a few. I've decided that I don't mind showing "sin" in a role that I accept. People sin. I believe every person does. That's what makes the stories told in theatre, film, and TV so human and so powerful to me—but I don't want to celebrate it. I want to show the real truth behind sinful choices: they destroy you and others.

Now, there are still things I, Actress Abbie Cobb, simply won't do onstage or on-camera, even if it is to preach an after-school special about the negative consequences of poor choices. For example, if my character is doing illegal drugs in a moving film about how drugs destroy lives, I would take the role. Would I actually take illegal drugs while filming? Or to help me "get into character?" No way! (Don't worry. You're not actually going to be asked to do illegal drugs for a scene. It's just an extreme example.) In other words, no matter how "positive" the message, there are still things I simply won't do as a person, even if it is "just acting."

I'm still learning about this gray area, sometimes the hard way. I've made mistakes and still have questions. I know that some people take this to the extreme one way or the other. Maybe they only do "Christian plays" or feel that acting is just pretending, so everything is fair game. I've shared with you the model I feel comfortable with. Also, I am thankful for the mentors I can call on for advice to keep the model on track. (Get some of those!) Be ready for the curveballs, even when you think you have it all figured out.

An Awakening

Let me give you another example from my own personal experience. When I first moved to LA, I had the opportunity to audition for the lead role of

Wendla in the play *Spring Awakening*. I had heard about the scandalous hit musical that rocked Broadway's socks off a few years prior, so I was hesitant. The musical adaptation of the German 1891 play gained infamy for pushing the envelope: onstage nudity and intimacy, pervasive profanity, etc. Probably not a show you'd see with Grandma. But this LA audition was a true-to-the-original adaptation of the 19th century play itself.

Understanding that this was a different production from the Broadway show, I did my homework. I checked out a copy of the play from the public library. (Remember those?) I read it cover to cover. And what did I find? A beautiful classic drama with turn-of-the-century costumes, language, and themes of repression and, ultimately, redemption. The play addresses timeless, complex questions. What happens when lies are told? What are the consequences of acting selfishly, lustfully? The play is full of consequences for bad choices: abortion, rape, and suicide, just to name a few.

This is an interesting situation. Here we have the same story with the same characters portrayed in very different ways. While the musical celebrates promiscuity and profanity, the play on which it's based takes a far more serious and realistic look at the consequences of poor choices. I would argue that the role of Wendla in the musical is very different from the original play. In the musical,

Wendla and Melchior rebel against their parents and and get into all kinds of shenanigans out of a sense of lust and rebellion. In the play, the choice is all Melchior's: Wendla is a victim of an assault. In the musical, Wendla is a willing and eager player in the rebellion. In the play, she is a sheltered, naïve victim. In both shows, Wendla gets pregnant and dies from the botched abortion her ashamed mother makes her get. This (among other things) leads Melchior to decide to commit suicide in the final scene. In the musical, Wendla's ghost appears, offering forgiveness and a final statement of stick-it-to-the-man, of their forbidden love rising above the times. In the original play, a masked man appears to Melchior and offers forgiveness as an alternative to suicide. He offers hope in the face of seeming hopelessness. The LA production's adaptation of the play that I was considering combined these endings. Like the musical, it is Wendla's ghost that appears. But, unlike the musical, her message is not one of rebellion being worth it. It is the masked man's message of forgiveness against all odds, of light in the darkness.

While the musical celebrates consensual teen sexuality and rocks out to the joys of nudity and cursing, the play offers a raw look at the harsh consequences of lies, lust, and assault, and in the end offers encouragement and a second chance to those who are broken.

Oh my goodness! If there was ever a piece of drama that points to exactly what I believe and would give me a chance to touch others through my art in a meaningful way, this was it! In the play, Wendla, a victim, forgives someone who doesn't deserve it. I went forward with the audition and was cast as Wendla.

Which leads me to my next point: be very careful before you judge someone for participating in a production that you have never seen. When I told people I was in *Spring Awakening,* a lot of people responded with a sense of judgment. All they knew about was the R-rated musical. Very few gave me the benefit of the doubt that I had done my research and carefully considered the heart of the story's message and its moral of forgiveness—and chosen to embrace it with confidence.

Stop Judging Other People

I had the privilege of being part of a Q&A panel about being a person of faith in the entertainment industry. A girl came up to me afterwards and said, "I've been talking it over with my mom, and I've set my standards. No cursing and no kissing!"

I asked her why she decided that kissing wasn't okay with her. She told me she is saving her first kiss for her wedding day, and she doesn't want to kiss anyone but her husband. I told her I didn't think that wanting to be a leading actress was a good idea then, explaining how most plays and movies involve love stories, most likely with kissing. I told her she might not be able to be an actress, or at least a leading lady, because of that decision.

At first I thought her decision was extreme, because her list was not the same as my own. Then I started thinking, "Wait, maybe that is wrong for her. Who am I to decide what is okay for her and what isn't?" What might be wrong for one person might not be wrong for another person. For example, a married person who has struggled with remaining faithful in their relationship might believe that kissing another person onstage or in film would lead to further struggles. That's way more important than any role. Your marriage is for life, but this role—and, yes, all the potential fame and fortune that may follow—is fleeting. On the other hand, maybe a married person who has done hundreds of kisses for stage and film sees it simply as choreography and his or her spouse is fine with it. Let me put it another way: A former alcoholic probably shouldn't have a glass of champagne at a wedding; at the same time, having a glass of celebratory champagne would likely be normal behavior for others who haven't struggled with alcohol abuse in the past. A person who struggles with violent thoughts may not want to play the latest shoot-'em-up video game, while playing the same game could be no problem for someone else without a violent past. It's not for us to say what others are allowed to participate in or shy away from in this gray area of "dos and don'ts." I believe that each actor is responsible for doing his or her own soul-searching based on the content of a part. The last thing in the world we should do is pelt our peers with accusations and judgments based on our own experience and our own decisions.

Recently, I was discussing this issue with an agent in LA who is a woman of faith. She told me about a client of hers, a (now famous) young woman who was up for the lead in a film that was centered around teen drinking. The studio offered her the role, but this actress wanted to decline the role because teen drinking was not something she wanted to endorse or encourage.

The agent said, "So, you're passionate about this subject and you care about this problem?"

"Exactly!" the actress replied.

The agent explained, "This movie is going to be made whether you're playing this role or not. Since young girls look up to you, wouldn't you rather have someone who cares about this issue take the role? You'd be the one giving the interviews. You'd be the one invited to speak about it. You'd be the one in the posters on their walls. Wouldn't it be better if it was you, the one who cares about the issue, speaking out against it, rather than an actress who is just excited to have a role and doesn't care about the content?"

In the right context, that's a good point. The actress ended up accepting the role and having a platform to speak on the subject, becoming a great role model for young teens everywhere. All those people who saw her on the movie poster (without even seeing the movie) and judged her for making a "bad choice" have no idea how much thought and care she put into accepting the role, thinking about the bigger picture.

Can I Get an "Amen"?

I believe in the power of prayer. As cliché as it sounds, I feel prayer is often the solution to any battle you face in this area of your career and your life. If, like me, you believe in a God who hears   prayers, then take my advice seriously. Pray for protection. If you're unsure about whether a role would hurt you or help you, pray about it! Start a conversation. If you believe in the same God I do, then you know He doesn't want us to be confused, and He certainly doesn't want us trapped in a scenario from which we can't escape.

173

I heard a story recently about a young man who turned to prayer after running into a sticky situation. He'd booked a guest-starring arc for three episodes on a TV series. He had only read the first episode, and it seemed harmless enough, so he signed the contract and legally committed himself to perform in all three episodes. However, when it came time for episode two, there were countless red flags flying high all over the place. He panicked. Much of what his character was to say and do directly conflicted with the standards he had set for himself. What was he to do? He couldn't break his contract, but he also didn't want to perform the actions asked of him.

And so he prayed. And, wouldn't you know it, this actor was from Mexico and it was discovered to everyone's surprise that his work visa expired just before the second episode was scheduled to begin filming. It is the producers' responsibility to check the workers' permits before hiring any actor, so they were the ones at fault. He was able to get out of the role without even bringing up the content issues with the producers at all.

Of course, this is a great example of the importance of going the extra mile to do your homework before accepting a role. But, to me, it's also a story of the power of prayer. It is never a waste of your time to ask for help. It will never be to your detriment to ask for wisdom. I believe that prayer works—and this gray area is too difficult to navigate alone. Trust me, you'll want all the help you can get.

What You Can Do Right Now

- o Do your soul searching. What do you believe and why?
- o Start making your list. What are your non-negotiables?
- o If you believe that prayer works, start getting in shape for the biggest prayer event of your life.
- o Check out the Hollywood Prayer Network (see next section) and get involved! Becoming a prayer partner for a person who is already working in Hollywood is a great way to get started.
- o If you plan to visit LA, make time in your schedule to scope out organizations (like the ones listed in the People You Should Know section of this chapter) where you can listen to experienced people of faith share their advice and insight.

The Time I Failed At...

One summer I was itching to do some theatre before the next school year began, so I browsed through the Arts and Entertainment section of the newspaper (back in the days when you actually had a giant folded stack of newsprint lying around your kitchen) and found a hilarious open-call audition for the workshop of a new musical.

The show? *Toxic Avenger: The Musical.* I knew nothing about the original movies on which this new play was based, but I went to the audition anyway, just to see what was up. They had sides in the lobby and I was there with my headshot and resumé, ready to take on the world. The lines were silly and the jokes were crass, but I chalked it up to "a comedy's a comedy" and knew that it was still in "workshop" mode, meaning the writer was working through a bunch of ideas before settling on anything in particular. Should've seen that red flag flying high.

I was called back the next day and offered the role of the lead "bad girl" who would be killed off halfway through the show, then I could double as a crazy librarian in the second act. What fun! What little research I did! And, oh, how sorry I was!

Only after I accepted the role did I take the time to check out the movies. Had I done so earlier, I would have realized it was chock-full of violence and crass sexual humor—not exactly my style. Yes, I'd read the scenes they provided to me and a few flags were raised, but I had brushed them aside, thinking it was a "working draft" and there would be changes.

Here's a hint: If you're ever concerned about content, never agree to a project that you haven't read completely. In my case, the ending wasn't written yet, but there were still questions I could have asked. What is the overall arc of my character? Any redeemable qualities to the story? Oh, none? Okay, thanks.

If you're auditioning for a play, always check the script out first and read it cover to cover. If you're auditioning for an independent film or a feature film, your agent will almost always have access to the script, and you can read it before you go in for the audition or before you get further along in the casting process. This way, you can gracefully bow out of a project before being cemented in the director's mind, which would prevent you from rocking the boat and burning a bridge.

In my *Toxic* situation, by the time I got all my lines (two months into rehearsal) and realized I didn't want the part, it was too late. I was stuck! If I stayed in the production, what was that saying about my faith and my values? However, if I backed out of the production and left my fellow artists stranded and unable to recast, what was that saying about my character and commitment? It was a lose/lose situation.

Word to the wise: don't be stupid. Read projects before you commit to them. If the script is unavailable and offers have been made, have a long chat with the casting director, director, or writer about the content and overall arc of your character. See what you can glean from the few pages you do have. What are the wardrobe notes? Is the dialogue hinting at any themes you're uncomfortable with? Better to do the homework now than quit a project—and never be cast by that director (and possibly the entire network) again.

People You Should Know

168 Hour Film Project
168 is an annual, worldwide filmmaking competition and exhibition. This is the challenge for filmmakers: Draw a random scripture and in just one week (168 hours), shoot and edit a short film. Their goal is to focus emerging filmmakers on excellence and the word of God.
Website: *www.168project.com*

Actors Co-op
Actors Co-op Hollywood is a professional theatre company made up of actors dedicated to excellence and building each other up spiritually, personally, and professionally in order to be an outreach of Christ's hope.
Website: *www.actorsco-op.org*

The Beacon
The Beacon is a community of Christian enter-tainment professionals seeking excellence in their crafts and serving others with their God-given gifts. They meet the 2nd and 4th Sunday of every month at Bel Air Presbyterian Church from 12:30-2 p.m. They usually alternate each session, with a speaker from the industry one week (screen writer, director, video game designer, actor, etc) followed by teaching and application from scripture the next week.

Website: *www.belairpres.org* (Click on "Connect and Grow," then "Entertainment Industry.")

The Bridge Entertainment Fellowship
They provide a time of prayer, personal sharing, Bible study and community in an environment where entertainment industry Christians can feel safe and supported. Their goal is to help unify the body of Jesus in the entertainment industry and to encourage Christians to commit and serve in the church body.
Website: *www.lakeave.org/ministries-a-to-z/the-bridge-entertainment-fellowship*

The Greenhouse
The greenhouse exists to bring artists to life. It seeks to maximize the potential and productivity of creative artists through mentoring, discussions, and artistic productions, and to equip artists to create excellent art and entertainment.
Website: *www.greenhouseproductions.com*

Hollywood Connect
Hollywood Connect equips and empowers industry believers spiritually, professionally and personally. They offer an extensive website, Hollywood orientation sessions, and various seminars/workshops. Hollywood Connect also believes in building relationships between the local body of Christ and the world.
Website: *www.hollywoodconnect.com*

Hollywood Prayer Network
HPN is a prayer ministry for the purpose of praying for the people, the projects, and the powerful influence of the global entertainment industry.
Website: *www.hollywoodprayernetwork.org*

Closing

At the top of that Ferris wheel that night—just me and my dummy—I realized something very important. When you're stuck on a ride, all thrill and amusement quickly fade. I didn't want it to be that way that night. I don't want that for my career. And I certainly don't want that for you.

I'd love to say that I climbed off my cart and started up the machinery to save myself, but that didn't happen. I'd love to brag about the way I leapt from my seat and deployed the parachute I'd tucked away for such emergencies. Of course, that didn't happen either. I ended up doing the smartest thing possible: getting help.

It took about two hours, but, eventually, my frantic shouts and waves and efforts were noticed and I was safely wheeled back to Earth with a bazillion apologies and some leftover spaghetti waiting for me.

Pursuing your dreams in Los Angeles is a wild ride. It's incredibly exciting. It's incredibly bumpy. At times, it is thrilling and, other times, scary. It's expensive. It's daunting. It's rewarding.

I really want you to enjoy this ride with me. It's unlike anything else you'd ever experience in the world. But it's also incredibly vital for you to get your feet planted on the ground physically, intellectually, and spiritually. Don't try to do this on your own! Reading books, like the one you're holding now, will only help you. Keep reading! Find a mentor. Take classes. Do your homework. Make your list.

And, by all means, buy some tickets for a carnival attraction or two.

You never know where the ride may take you.

Glossary

2nd 2nd is the assistant to the assistant director's assistant. (Got that?) They are normally in charge of all background actors (extras), including handing out SAG vouchers, firing unruly extras, etc. Every show and film works a little differently, but if there are no extras for production that day, the 2nd 2nd is usually in charge of base camp.

2nd AD is the assistant to the assistant director. They typically stand near the director to delegate tasks and communicate the AD or director's needs to the people who can make it happen. Certain films or shows will have the 2nd AD running base camp.

Actor's Access (actorsaccess.com) is the version of Breakdowns that any Joe Schmoe in Hollywood can see. Actors are not privy to the direct access that representation has to Breakdowns, but we can have access to our account on this site, adding and updating headshots, reels, resumés, etc. There is a fee to add pictures and have an account on Actor's Access, but it is absolutely necessary.

Actor's Equity Association (AEA) is the union for actors who are working in professional theatre. You can earn points and join Equity by being hired at an Equity-sanctioned theatre or cast in an Equity production. You can also buy membership to Actor's Equity if you are a member of one of their sister unions, including SAG, for one year.

Agent is responsible for submitting actors to casting directors for consideration. They get auditions for the actors by submitting an electronic (or sometimes hard copy) version of your headshots and resumé. They make phone calls and send emails on behalf of the actor if they feel you are particularly perfect for a specific role, and "pitch" you to the casting director. An agent is a major form of representation.

Alternate List is the sign-in sheet for non-Equity actors at an Equity theater audition. If Equity actors cancel their audition or auditions are running ahead of schedule, the monitor can start calling actors in from the alternate list.

Assistant Director (AD) is the second-in-command who puts into action the requests of the director and the director of photography (DP) and oversees the crew. The immediate tasks that the AD performs or delegates frees up the director to work individually with actors, watch playback, etc. Do whatever he or she says promptly and with a smile on your face. So from the top down, following the director, the AD positions are: AD, 2nd AD, 2nd 2nd.

Background/Extras work for a TV show or movie to help set the scene behind the main actors who have been cast in the production. Any role that doesn't speak and usually doesn't interact with the main character is an extra. You usually don't have to audition for background roles.

Backstage West is a publication that I recommend every actor subscribe to online. You pay a totally affordable subscription fee twice a year and gain access to hundreds of articles, audition notices, and networking ads. They have audition postings organized in a way where you can select the category you're auditioning for and an area of the country and all the latest auditions will come up with detailed information on how to submit for each role.

Barcode represents your digital commercial profile. A commercial casting director can scan your barcode (literally on a piece of paper you're holding) and see your resumé, headshot, etc. on their computer.

Base Camp is the center of production and is manned at all times, often by the 2nd 2nd or a PA. This is where the actors' trailers, mealtimes, etc.

are located. There is someone here with a radio to communicate between the current shooting location and the behind-the-scenes departments, such as make-up, wardrobe, etc.

Bodyshot is a picture or camera angle of you from head to toe.

Breakdown is a term for the specific roles and character descriptions needed for any project (film, modeling, theatre, etc.) It is where a casting director will "break down" what is needed for each character, such as body type, age, gender, etc. For example, "Can you send me the character breakdown so I can decide what I should wear to my audition?"

Breakdowns (breakdownservices.com) is the online forum for casting directors to post what specific roles they're looking for at breakdownservices.com. Only agents and managers have access to this website. The version of this site for actors is *actorsaccess.com*. For example, "Can you look at Breakdowns and find Project A to see if there is a potential role for me?"

Callback is the second round of auditions. They take place following the first audition, also called pre-reads, and include the head casting director and possibly another decision maker, like a director.

Call-in Service is a company that you hire to get background jobs for you. Most require a monthly fee of $40-60 dollars, depending on the company. This is especially helpful if you are working background full-time because you are often stuck on set and can't call to get work for the next day. These services will submit you for projects you appear right for and will call you with details for the job if you are booked.

Call Time is the time you are given to show up on the production set.

Casting Director is hired by the producer or director to cast all roles in the show. The producer and directors will have a say on the large roles, but the options are brought to them by the casting director(s). Even one-line actors have to be cast and usually it's a waste of time for the director to do it himself. Casting directors interview for their position just like actors do; many are considered and only one gets the job.

Casting Office is a company with one or more casting directors that have been hired to find actors/models for a particular project.

Central Casting is a casting agency that works exclusively for background actors with most major TV shows and feature films. You must make an appointment to enroll, where they'll take a photo of you and put it in their computer system. TV shows will hire Central Casting to provide them with background actors. For example, *NCIS* might say, "We need to fill a mall with 30 upscale mall shoppers." Central Casting will then make a recording on a telephone line saying, "Filming tomorrow, Monday, February 13th, *NCIS* production is looking for 30 shoppers, male or female between the ages of 17 and 55. Call extension 3445 if you fit this description." Sounds pretty universal, right? The casting director will either listen to their voicemails and choose the first thirty that he feels fits the description or answer the phone themselves and chat with you and tell you whether you're booked or not.

Chemistry Read is one of the final steps of major audition processes that is meant to determine which actors mesh the best with others. For example, it might be new actors coming into an existing cast or mixing-and-matching couples to find two new romantic leads.

Co-star is an actor who typically has around five lines or less on a TV production.

Craigslist.com is a free online classifieds website with apartments, jobs, items for sale etc.

Find potential small-time jobs on your town's page under "Gigs."

Dayplayer is an actor who typically has around five lines or less on a film and is working for one day.

Demo (Reel) is a video or audio montage to act as an electronic resumé.

Director of Photography (DP) is in charge of the look and feel of a film or TV show and responsible for setting the shot, determining lighting, etc. They do not interact with actors a great deal but ,rather, focus on setting the visual mood of a scene.

Equity is the term for being in the theatre union, Actors Equity' Association (AEA). For example, "Are you Equity?" means "Are you in the theatre union AEA?"

Equity Card is the membership card to the union with your ID number on it.

Equity Membership Candidate (EMC) is an actor who has not officially joined AEA but has begun accruing points towards their union membership. An actor who has accrued enough points for membership but has not joined is considered EMC.

Equity Principal Audition (EPA) is an audition for a union, or Equity, show for a lead (principal) role.

Extra *See Background/Extras*

Financial Core is a union status you can choose to take if you aren't finding enough work and want to temporarily be non-union to find more work. There are some benefits to doing this if you find yourself in a tough place, but it is never recommended. An actor must pay back-dues when they wish to re-join, and it's seen as a sign that the actor was not talented enough to make it in the union.

First Team is the group of principal actors on set required for the filming scheduled that day. The AD will often shout out which team is needed for filming that is happening right then. Stand-ins, photo doubles, etc. are considered second team.

Frame refers to the size of the shot you're standing in, according to what camera lens sees. If the frame is tight, that usually means the lens is zoomed way in and only your neck and face are on camera. If the frame is wide, that may mean your whole body is in the shot. It's helpful to know what your frame is when you audition so you know if any movement is necessary.

Obviously, if the frame is tight, you won't need to pantomime, worry about where your script is, or move like you planned when you rehearsed the night before. If the frame they give you is wider than your whole body, you know you have the freedom to sit down, turn around, pretend to eat, etc.

Guest Star is an actor billed higher than a co-star with a larger supporting role in the TV show with multiple lines and/or scenes.

Headshot is an 8x10 photograph of your face, representing one of your types as an actor printed in color. It can also be in digital form for online use.

LaCasting.com is the commercial version of Breakdowns. Commercial casting directors who are working on a Pepsi commercial or Super Bowl spot or PSA (public service announcement), etc., post the roles they're casting online, and your commercial agent can submit you via electronic link. Again, it costs money to have an account online, but it is completely worth it; you may not ever get an audition at all if you don't have an account with pictures on this website.

Manager is a form of representation and your personal cheerleader! Managers can get you auditions, but their primary role is to manage your career. They do everything from helping you choose an outfit for an audition to scrutinizing your headshots to negotiating contracts. They typically only have a few actors, or clients, so they have more time to devote individual attention to you.

Mark refers to the spot you're supposed to stand on when you're in a scene. It can be a piece of tape on the floor of an audition room, or it could be a rock you're supposed to feel with your feet on a film set. A director may say, "hit this mark by this line," so the cameramen will know where you are going to be and so you'll know where to stand (to make sure you don't go out of frame). Almost all filmed auditions will have a taped mark on the floor for you to stand on.

Monitor is the person helping run Equity auditions. They are the person to see about signing in or answer any questions you might have. They typically arrive to the audition 30-60 minutes before it begins.

Networks are the head honchos that call the shots and make billions of dollars. You'll know them as ABC, Disney, CNN, FOX, USA, Showtime, etc.

Non-union means you are not a member of SAG/ AFTRA, AEA, etc. Non-union members do not get the same benefits that union members do, but they do make at least the minimum wage of the state they're working in for background/extra work. Typically there are more non-union jobs available, although they will not pay as much.

Network Test is the furthest you can go in the audition process, when you audition for the producers' bosses, such as the head(s) of a network like CBS.

Off-Camera the action, person, etc. that is not seen by the audience (and camera angle) but is "seen" by the actor onscreen.

PA *See Production Assistant*

Photo Double resembles one of the first team actors enough to substitute for them in certain scenes, such as a shot of a hand writing a letter or dialing a phone number. They are considered second team.

Pilot is the first episode of a new show that will often be tested with various audiences before a network will sign (and finance) a show for more episodes.

Pilot Season is the busy time of year when networks are casting the first episodes of new shows: the pilots. The primary pilot season runs from mid-January through mid-April, but several are also cast from mid-August to mid-November.

Producer is the money-manager/financier for any production. It's their job to know how much money is spent on what; they're in charge of penny pinching or giving the a-okay to spend, spend, spend. Since they're either the financiers themselves or working directly with the people who have the moolah to back a production, they usually have the final say when it comes to casting or other big decisions (location, script ideas, etc.).

Producer Session is a step further than a callback; producers are in attendance at the audition, which may or may not be followed by a chemistry read, screen test, or network test.

Production Assistant (PA) is on the bottom of the production totem pole, doing tasks delegated to them by the 2nd 2nd or higher, such as escorting actors to set, faxing scripts, running to Starbucks, etc.

Recurring Role is a character that spans over more than one episode in a TV series, including a recurring guest star or co-star.

Reel *See Demo*

Representation is the term for an agent or a manager who represents you as their client. For example, "Do you have representation?" means "Do you have an agent or a manager?"

Resumé is a document where all your industry experience is located, including information like your name, body stats, previous roles, contact info, representation info, etc.

SAG/AFTRA (Screen Actors Guild/American Federation of Television and Radio Artists) is the biggest union that represents actors for film and television. These two groups were once separate but merged into one giant performer's union in 2011. You qualify to be a union actor if you have had lines on a TV show or movie, or you have earned three SAG vouchers by being an extra on a union TV show or movie. It currently costs $2,400 to join the union, and there are bi-annual dues.

SAG-E (SAG-Eligible) means you've earned yourself a spot in SAG/AFTRA but, for some reason, have chosen to wait to pay your dues to join. This could be because you don't have the money or you want to get more non-union work on your resumé. "Taft Hartley" is when you are non-union and are hired anyway (or given a line) for a union project. Being "Taft-Hartlied" or "getting a Taft Hartley" makes you SAG-Eligible.

Screen Test is a final on-set audition that could act as a chemistry read between candidates for a role and the actors already hired. This helps producers, network execs, etc., see which actors best fit the role when they're actually on a set, with hair/makeup done, wardrobe, lighting, etc.

Script Supervisor follows along in the script during filming to correct line mistakes, add last-minute line additions from the writers, etc. They are available to run lines with you and can either be your best friend or your worst nightmare, depending on how good you are at memorizing. They are in charge of continuity and will also keep a note of which scenes the director wants to "print," or keep for the editors. Also known as "the Scripty."

Second Team is a group of stand-ins or body doubles who often physically resemble the main actors they represent. Second team members never have lines in the final edit. The AD will often shout out which team is needed before the setup and filming of each shot begins.

Showcase is an event to display your talents, and possibly compete with your peers, for a panel of judges. Entry fees are usually involved.

Sides are an excerpt of a script with your lines for filming/auditions and are provided for you on set if you book the job. A side can be any-where from 1 page to 30 pages. It's the portion of the script that is necessary for that moment. When you're on set, the PAs will hand out sides and those sides contain every line and action to be filmed that day. If you have a big audition, the Casting Director may email you sides to prepare - not necessarily the whole script, just the few pages you need to know to get an idea of what the character is like and what you need to read for them during the audition.

Slate "Giving a slate" or "slating your name" is the term given to the first few seconds of a recorded audition where you say your name for the camera and any details that the producer or casting director may ask of you. The purpose of a slate is so people watching the playback of an audition can identify who you are.

Spec is when an actor arrives at a production set in the hopes that a background actor will not show up and a replacement will be needed.

Stand-In stands in the place of a principal actor they resemble while the crew uses them to set up lighting, props, etc. They are considered second team.

Storyboard is similar to a comic book strip and contains several illustrations in the correct order of events to depict what will take place (what the audience will see) in a movie or commercial.

Survival Job is the job you have in addition to acting that pays your bills and allows you the flexibility to audition for roles.

"Taft Hartley" is when you are non-union and are hired anyway (or given a line) for a union project. Being "Taft-Hartlied" or "getting a Taft Hartley" makes you SAG/AFTRA Eligible.

Type(s) is the category (or stereotype) of people in which an actor can fit him or her self, such as cheerleader, dad, prison guard, babysitter, jock, grandma, etc.

Video Village is the on-set location where all the camera footage can be seen simultaneously while filming. A video monitor is set up with chairs in front of it for the director, director of photography, writer, script supervisor, executive producers, and first team actors. Everyone watches with headphones during filming from this location except for the camera operators, including hair and make-up crew.

Voiceover is a type of work where your voice is recorded for any type of media (TV, film, web, or radio) or product (videogame, audiobook, child's toy, etc.)

Voucher System is the process of earning your way into SAG by having the opportunity to sign three yellow official SAG vouchers.

Wardrobe Notes are the details of a character given in a breakdown that describes what that character would be wearing. These are helpful when preparing for auditions.

About the Author

Abbie Cobb is an actor who is currently in the trenches, learning every day from her successes and mistakes. She recurred on the popular ABC series *Suburgatory* and also co-starred in the feature film *Mom's Night Out*. Most recently, she starred in the ABC drama pilot *Warriors* and CW's *Cheerleader Death Squad* and has had recurring roles on both CW's *90210* and ABC Family's *Secret Life of the American Teenager.*

After landing her very first role on Disney's *Starstruck* she continued working with Disney on shows like *Pair of Kings, Good Luck Charlie: It's Christmas, Jonas LA,* and *Imagination Movers.* She eventually moved on to guest star on other networks in shows like *American Horror Story, NCIS:LA and :NewOrleans, Grey's Anatomy, The Mentalist,* and *Criminal Minds.* She enjoys filling up her weeks with work in TV, film, or theatre, but she also knows how hard it is to break into acting so she spends her spare time sharing what she has learned from the process.

Abbie currently lives and works in LA. She still drives her pick-up truck from Nebraska.

Follow her journey at abbiecobb.com
Instagram: Abbiecobb
Twitter: @thelovelyabs